REMEMBER

THE

LILIES

a military mom's journey

REMEMBER

THE

LILIES

learning to release
the power of Heaven
over our children

SHERRY MOTCHECK

Cover photo by Ashley Sietsema @Simply Unique Photography
Cover Design & Interior by Sarah O'Neal @Eve Custom Artwork
Peony Vector courtesy of AdobeStock

Published by Tinder Mountain Press L.L.C

Printed in the U.S.A.

For More Information &
To purchase The book please visit
sherrymotcheck.com

My sons, Adam and Matthew, because of you, my heart has found the beat of a warrior. Because of you, I am more. May you always know that Jesus and your mama are forever on your team and always with you on the front lines. I am so very proud of you both. This is our story. Thank you for letting me share it...

as big as the sky

My husband, Michael, you are my reward, my blessing, and the reflection of God's love for me. Thank you for cheering me on, believing in me, pushing me forward, and praying me through this wild adventure of life. You are forever my best thing...

Just you and me babe

My children's children, you are in my heart even now, though you are not yet here on earth. Within the pages of this book, you will find the story of your daddy and me and Jesus. May it open the vault in Heaven where you will find your Kingdom inheritance is waiting for you. I pray you step into a legacy that lets you run further than I ever will or could...

as big as the sky

"We were fashioned to be
powerful women of God
armed with the weaponry of heaven.

acknowledgments

To Margaret Wrasse—My editor. Thank you for all of the hours pouring over this book. You took the words from my heart and reassembled them in order to articulate what I could not. Your encouragement, direction, wisdom, and endless patience along the way made this book take flight. May God repay you one hundred twenty fold what you lent out to me. I am forever grateful.

To the reader, please note that Margaret allowed me creative freedom to let this book read as if you were sitting having a cup of coffee with me and listening to my stories. All fragment sentences, mixtures of past and present tenses, grammatical errors from storytelling are entirely my doing. I'm a rebel that way.

To Debi Lowe—My mama, Lyndzie Motcheck, Terry Yax, Bailee Shepler, Maddy Motcheck, and Corrine Cockream—my tribe. The women who know my heart the best. Thank you for being the guinea pigs and reading through all the jumble to find the pith of this book. Your input and your honesty made this ready for the masses.

To Emery Lowe—My daddy. Thank you for instilling in me patriotism and love of country and for letting me share a portion of your story in the pages of this book. You are forever my hero!

To Ashley Sietsema—My patient, brilliant photographer who is always there to capture the essential moments in my life. Thank you for the incredible cover photo and for helping me recreate Matthew 6:28's "lilies of the field" using shipped-in flowers and my son's actual military boots. You did it! It's stunning.

To Sarah O'Neal—My book designer. Wow! You caught my vision and heartbeat and created something so beautiful. Your talent is bar none, and I am so thankful to have you on my team.

To the crew in Texas—The group of guys that fell backward into becoming my copy editors, thank you! You were amazing. You smoothed out the edges and gave this story some polish. You also let me see just how far God could reach with the pages of this book.

preface

Before we dive into the crux of this book, I feel it is necessary to first establish who God created us to be as women. To do that, we have to go back all the way to the garden for you to see just how powerful you are.

The Lord God said, "It is not good for the man to be alone. I will make a helper suitable for him."

GENESIS 2:18

We are going to be looking at the word "helper" in this text. The word "helper" here in the NIV translation can also be found as "help meet" in the KJV. We need to remember that the original scriptures were written in Hebrew, and sometimes even when the greatest minds come together to translate, things still get lost in translation. When we look at the words of scripture as it was written in the original Hebrew language, we get a deeper understanding. Looking up this particular verse in the original Hebrew language, the word "helper" is actually ezer. *I will make an ezer suitable for him.* When you load that word ezer into a Bible search, you will find that it is used twenty-one times in the Old Testament. What may surprise you as you look at the places it is used in scripture is that God not only used that word to describe the attributes of a woman when she was created, but He also uses that word to describe Himself! Here are some passages where God uses ezer in scripture to describe Himself.

There is no one like the God of Jeshurun, who rides across the heavens to help (ezer) you and on the clouds in his majesty.

DEUTERONOMY 33:26

The Lord is their/our help (ezer) and our shield.

PSALM 33:20 & PSALM 115:9, 10, 11

And the other one was named Eliezer, for he said, "My father's God was my helper (ezer) and saved me from the sword of Pharaoh.

EXODUS 18:4

This last passage references Moses naming his son Eliezer which means God is my help.

So, what does ezer actually mean? It means: to rescue, to save, to be strong. It is often used as God being an ezer to mankind and is mentioned during times of battle or war or conflict. Moses was saved from Pharaoh's sword more than once when God showed up as ezer. It's a powerful military term. Ezer describes God as a warrior. It's that same powerful word God assigned to describe women. Not only was it our destiny to come alongside our husbands and be all the things he was not created to be, but

God put within women His warrior attributes! He is *our help and shield*. What is a shield for? To block the blows of the enemy. Are you listening? God put within you the power to block the blows of the enemy in battle! You are not helpless! You are not cast aside as your children embark on this journey. They need you more than ever. You just need to see yourself as the warrior God created you to be.

There is another scripture I would like to show you.

The Lord will create a new thing on earth-the woman will return to the man.

JEREMIAH 31:22

If we look this verse up in its original text, the word return is sabab in Hebrew, which means encompass, surround, encircle, to turn about, change, transform. The word man in this verse is geber, and it means a valiant man or warrior.

The woman, who has the attributes of a warrior, will encompass, surround, change, and transform a valiant man or warrior! That is who you are! Warrior is part of our identity as women. We are designed to be fighters. We are created to be on the front lines. God wants to show us a new thing. He wants to do a new thing as we step into our calling to surround and help and protect our warriors! Maybe you are saying, "I have no idea what that looks like!" You'd be right, because it's going to be new. And YOU are going to do it.

I believe that those of us who have been given the honor of holding the position of Military Mom have been put in this place because we have been given a great anointing to be modern-day, Spirit-filled, Shield-maidens. This is what I have come to see us becoming in the Spirit. Shield-maidens are women who choose to fight. They want to fight. They carry the courage and weapons of Heaven. They are clothed in His armor and righteousness, and they run straight to the front lines of battle, fully intent on not leaving their post until a victory comes forth. I see us all in a battle formation standing side by side in our armor with swords and shields that deflect the enemy in hand having faces set like flint as we advance and take the land with the same power that rose Christ from the grave living in us. We are mothers of children serving this nation. We are called to rise up and stand in the gap on their behalf and on behalf of those serving with them. We are called to be their help and shield. We are called to be watchmen on the wall, to pull down Heaven and fight for them and with them as they fight for us. The gifts and callings He has put on your life since before you ever came to be here on this earth and before you ever took a breath will never go void. He will never call them back. He will never change his mind. Sister, you were chosen to be a military mom since the dawn of creation!

... for God's gifts and his call are irrevocable.

ROMANS 11:29

It's been said that military families are part of the silent rank, but I believe there should be *nothing* silent about us. It's time for us to make some noise in the heavenlies, call down Kingdom truth, and ring the Holy victory bell by using the open Heaven and the attributes that God has given us as women when He molded us with His own two hands. We are called to war and to pray on behalf of the military, not only on behalf of our children. While our children may be the catalyst that gets us there, our calling is much bigger. You will see that as you cover your child in prayer, you are also covering fellow servicemen and women, our president, our nation, and even other countries. You will be shielding them all from the enemies' blows.

Walking out this path that was put before me as a military mom has made me realize this has been my call to action. Though at times I feel far too small to be able to walk this calling out, I have to remember that God has already equipped me for this, and with every step, I only get stronger. He put into me His warrior traits, and He is wanting to do a new thing through me as I surround my sons. I have an anointing to forward their journey and even turnabout or change their courses as I push through in prayer. This is why I am writing this book. I believe this is your call to action as well. We are in this together. The reality that I am joining hearts and prayers with other warrior military moms across this amazing nation is so humbling and also a great privilege. Who am I that I should be chosen to be part of such a mighty force? It's such an amazing honor. I am stronger because of you. May we never forget how powerful we are together.

Then God Made Woman

Then God made you!

chapters

a note

Hi mama!

If you are holding this book in your hand, it probably means you are either about to be or are already fully inducted into the privileged position of Military Mom. As a mom who has had both of her sons in the military at the same time, I have been where you stand. I have felt everything you are feeling. It's a lot. It's overwhelming at times. I want to tell you that you are not alone. There are literally thousands of other moms walking through the very same thing you are. Unfortunately, when I first went through it, I did feel alone. I did not know one other mother who had one child in the military, let alone two.

Also, in all my searching, I could not find a devotional that would address the heart matters that I was experiencing as a new military mom. When I sat at my oldest son's PIR (Pass In Review- better known as boot camp graduation) from the United States Navy, I looked out at all the recruits, all lined up in their dress blues, and I realized that if the Navy is processing 500 graduates every single Friday, there were a lot of moms out there going through what I was going through. I just had to find them. I never wanted another military mom ever to feel isolated the way that I had. That passion, along with the unrelenting prompting of the Holy Spirit to share my journey, has led to this book.

I pray that through reading my personal memoir, excerpts from exchanged boot camp letters, along with the Word of God, and lessons He revealed to me along my journey, that you too will find strength, be encouraged, and find empowerment during this season in your life. When I first stepped into this role, I was lost. I was tattered. I was unsure. I did not feel very strong, and I certainly did not feel ready or even able to do this. Allowing God to lead me through it not only held me together but led me to find my strength. I was able to see and grab ahold of the anointing He has placed in my life for such a time as this. As you read my story, you will see that in my weakness, His strength made me strong. None of this is exclusive to me. My intent is that this book helps to get you there too. I pray that you will hear God's voice and realize your incredible anointing as a military mom.

You can do this! I know right now you may not feel like it, but you have been strategically placed right where you are. This position isn't for wimps. Remember, not every mom gets this honor, but you have! If you find yourself in this position, it's because you are stronger than you know. After all, you raised a Soldier, a Sailor, a Marine, an Airman, or a Coast Guardsman! There is something super powerful in just that alone, but there is so much more!

This is only the beginning. There is a revelation to come, things He has yet to reveal to you as you walk down this road. Whatever God gives to you along this journey, I encourage you to write it down. Be empowered to grab hold of other military moms you meet along the way and call them up to their rightful place. You will lead others that come after you that will walk this same journey. Let's make some noise and become a force to be reckoned with as we link arms together.

At the end of every chapter, I have given room for you to journal, reflect on given scriptures, and hear God speak to you as He spoke to me. Use that space however you need to in order to get your battle plan ready. Write, draw, dream, and do whatever you feel led to do as you sit and spend time with the Lord. When we write things down, we are able to go back and see how God has and is still moving. Sometimes writing, brings things out of our hearts we did not know were there. I find as I journal, God speaks to me through the words as I put pen to paper. I am not sure what will come out of the quiet time you spend with the Lord, but I know it will be powerful and life-changing, so write it down.

Then the Lord replied: Write down the revelation
and make it plain on tablets so that a herald
(or whoever reads it) may run with it.
For the revelation awaits an appointed time;

HABAKKUK 2:2-3

God has a plan for you and for your children. Scripture tells us that the steps of the righteous are ordered and planned by God (paraphrased from Psalm 37:23). He is always planning for our good and for the good of our children. Today, part of His plan is that He wants to talk with you. He has so much He wants to tell us; we just have to still ourselves and listen. I am praying that you find Him in a new way as you walk in this new role. I am so excited for what He is about to reveal to you, show you, awaken in you, arise in you, and release in you. You are a strong, powerful woman of God, and you were born to do this! You are equipped to do this. You were called for this very moment! Hang on, ladies! This is going to be an amazing ride.

I have been praying for you since I first put pen to paper, and I am praying for you still. Please know what an honor it is for me to be covering and warring for you and your children in prayer. I am standing alongside you, all the way. Come on, mama's, let's do this!

~Sherry

WHIPLASH & BLESSING

I CAUGHT THE FIRST GLIMPSE that I might be traveling down the unknown road of military mom three months before my oldest son Adam was finishing up his first year of college. He was attending school three hours away from home on a full scholarship for a music degree. He had picked up a guitar at a young age and figured out that music was his thing. From there, he taught himself to play various instruments, and now he was heading towards a career in something he loved.

When he came home for spring break, everything we thought we knew about where he was heading was completely unraveled. The little figurative box I had already organized and packed for his future suddenly sprung open, and its contents were dumped out, scrambled up, and rearranged with six words.

He sat us down and said, "I want to join the Navy." Now, you have to understand this child had never, not once, mentioned at any time in his life that this would be something he wished to pursue. He was my music child. He was also my careful child. He never leaped until he knew he'd be safe. He wasn't a risk-taker. He always made and had a plan. So, as you can imagine, this was more than a surprise. As the words were coming out of his mouth, I couldn't string them together in a way that made sense. It was like I was coming out of anesthesia, and the brain fog was too thick to see or hear through the haze. What on earth was he saying? This couldn't be Adam! He doesn't do things like this. Matthew, yeah, this would make sense. He's our wild card son, but not Adam! This couldn't be happening. How could this child have switched gears so quickly without me ever realizing or noticing that he was considering this?

As the brain fog slowly cleared and I could finally form human words, I began to ask questions. All of them. Everything I could think of to try and put the pieces together. As Adam began to answer, I watched the son I knew him to be, return. Even though the proposed change of career path had felt like whiplash and completely out of character for him, the thought process, the self-preparedness, and the planning, that was all him. It was then I knew I was in trouble. He had an answer to every single question. Not one question his father or I asked him had stumped him. There was no hesitation on any answer. He didn't pause to reflect or need time to think. He was concise, articulate, and sure. Every angle or circumstance we threw at him, he had already thought through. He had put in the time; he'd completed the research. He was making sure that when he leaped, he'd have a safe landing.

Well, you all know what I had to do. I had no choice! I had to play the godly mother card! You know the one we play when we need it to go away for a minute? The card that buys us time because we have no idea how to respond or what to say, but we don't want them to know that we might not be the all-knowing, wise parent? That card. The "I need time to pray about it" card. Wow. This was too much of a shock to the system. I had to find my breath. Not only did we as parents need a minute to process this, but my immediate inner prayer was that if I put him on hold, perhaps, he would change his mind. Or God would.

As we ended this conversation, my husband and I told him that he needed to finish up his year of school. He was getting exceptional grades, he had scholarships to cover the semester, and he had to finish strong. We agreed that we would pray about what he had shared with us during the next three months. Then, when school was out, and he was home for the summer, we would reconvene. Hopefully, this whole thing would be gone by then, but if not, I had plan B. I also added one more contingency for good measure. I told them that Adam couldn't move on anything until all three of us - Adam, his father, and myself were all in agreement. If it were God's plan, we would all hear the same thing.

Now, y'all, this wasn't a spiritual insight at all. At least, I didn't think so at the time. It was mainly another way to foil this absurd military idea. If he and his father actually did come back with a yes, and I came back with a no, he wouldn't be able to go. Right? I had three months to pray and ask God to change this kid's mind. Sheesh, I'd even throw in a fast if I had to. But even if he didn't change his mind, I had the contingency agreement card on the table. After all, I was never going to agree to this. I was desperate to get this kid back on track, repack this future box he'd just dumped all over the place and see him continue in his music career. I had no qualms whatsoever on being the mean parent and not being in agreement in order to stop him from going if I had to.

We sent him back to finish the school year, and the three-month countdown clock started. During that time, we prayed individually and together that God would give us direction and clarification about the steps He had ordered for our oldest son. When I was alone, I was secretly praying for

God to make this nonsense go away. It had to go away for so many reasons. The biggest one was knowing he would be willing to lay his life down for his county.

At this point, I feel I need to add a disclaimer in hopes that you can look through my lens and see my motivations and reasoning a little clearer. I am so proud to be an American. My daddy is a Viet Nam Veteran. My granddaddy served in WWII. I have uncles and nephews who are serving or have served in the military. I absolutely love this country. There is not one time that I see Old Glory flying with her beautiful red, white and blue colors that the meaning and sacrifice of my freedom is wasted on me. I am humbled and forever grateful to live in this country and honor our flag, whose colors don't run, and our military, whose bravery bought my freedoms. America, home of the free because of the brave. Patriotism is woven into the tapestry of who I am.

However, when it comes to handing your son over to Uncle Sam to become one of the brave, knowing he may full well come back in a flag-draped casket, that's a whole other level of patriotism. Agreeing to your child's increased risk of death does not sound like fun, and it goes against everything a mother's love is. I could not see how I could ever agree to this. But, as time stretched out and as fervent as my prayers and fasting were against it, I realized God was depositing in me a type of calm I'd never known before. I didn't like that joining the military was even a thought, let alone now becoming a possibility. I didn't understand it. I didn't want it. However, deep in my spirit, there was a heavenly deposit being made. It was peace; A peace that surpasses understanding. Sometimes you have to fight for peace. I write about that very fight in the Rock and Lilies chapter of this book. But then there are times that God will release this peace that surpasses understanding without warning so you can see His goodness and His hand moving. I was being stubborn and was not at all interested in seeing God move if He wasn't moving MY way. I cannot explain how it came to be, but strangely, I realized that I had total peace with the notion of my son joining the military. With that peace, I was able to see a little clearer. I knew that even though I hated it, and oh man did I hate it, I was going to have to let him go.

When the time had run out, and the three months had passed, it was just as I knew it would be. We reconvened at the end of his school year, we shared our hearts and our prayers, and it was crystal clear where Adam's next steps would take him. Adam was going directly to the United States Navy recruiter's office.

When Adam and Matthew were little, I realized that I could emotionally cripple my boys if I did not let them grow up, be independent, learn new things, and be without me for periods of time. As much as I hated them growing up, I knew that I was helping fulfill God's purpose and design for their lives by encouraging them to reach their next milestones. I had to put my own emotions and feelings aside and help spur them forward and on to victory. There was a time I remember when I stood with one of my little boys, his tiny hand hanging onto mine, and together we looked up at the big, big slide. We'd always gone down together. Now I was asking him to go alone. He was unsure and maybe even scared. Looking down at his little face, seeing his eyes searching mine, feeling his little hand squeeze a little tighter, I knew he would not go forward without me telling him he could do it, assuring him that I believed in him and that I'd be right there the whole time. It was my response to him and to the situation that would help him decide if he would succeed in climbing up the mountain-sized slide before him and then stick the landing at the end.

It was my honor as his mother to help him succeed. I was also keenly aware that two things were about to happen should he do this alone. The first is that once he realized he could do this without me, I would never slide down together with my little boy again. That season of him needing me for that portion of his life would be forever over. As heartbreaking as I found this first truth to be, the second truth was that my mama's heart was going to soar because he was able to do it alone. That's a mother's blessing. It's not the same bold, outspoken blessing we see David give to his son Solomon in 1 Kings 2. It's much softer than that but still so very powerful. Sometimes without realizing it, we have given our blessing while they are growing up. Throwing out the pacifier. Letting them ride the school bus. Driving the car without a parent. Each of the times I may have hated to see a season or phase come to an end, I inherently knew my sons were ready for the next stage. I knew they had to do it. If they fell off their bike and skinned a knee, I'd bandage them up, set them back on that bike, coach them up for success, and make them try again, until finally, they were able to ride their shiny new bikes in victory. There were many tears from me as they got dropped off at daycare, went away to summer camp, and decided they no longer wanted to marry me. It's hard to watch them grow up. It is. It happens way too fast, and the years flash by in a blink. But they had to do it, and I had to help them get there.

A mother's blessing is believing they can accomplish more than they believe they can accomplish and then nudging them forward to do it, even when we hate it. It's letting them take their own route, blaze their own trail, and get it done their own way. A mother's blessing is being there to pick up the pieces should they stumble and then standing them back up to do it again, knowing they may fall a second time. It is trusting that God has ordained their steps, and He will get them to where they need to be without me, even when I don't understand where or why they are going.

There are places I cannot physically go with my children, but when I give them my blessing, they take me with them. I was giving a mother's blessing while my children were growing up, even though I never realized that's what it was. Throughout it all, year after year, they have needed my blessing to get to the next stage or place in life. This was the revelation revealed to me during those three months of fervently praying against God's plan for my son's life. Yeah, I know, that last sentence alone will disqualify me from the mother-of-the-year award.

In sharing his new dream of joining the Navy with me, my son was seeking his mother's blessing even if those words were never vocalized. I never realized the power of a mother's blessing until this moment. He knew this was a big, HUGE ask, and he knew my mother's heart would be stretched further than it had ever been. Here he was, standing still in this place, his eyes searching mine, and he could not move forward without my blessing, just like the day looking at the slide. The terms get greater, the choices and decisions get more complex, but the power of the blessing remains the same. I really don't know if he would have gone without my blessing. I've never asked him. But I am forever grateful that God changed my heart so he would never have to make that choice. I want you to know that your blessing over your sons and daughters can catapult them straight onto their God-ordained path, or, without it, you could cripple them by holding them back.

Now I am not saying that I always agree with my children. Have I told them no before? Yes. Oi! There were many a time my boys called me the Death Star from Star Wars because I "blew up their dreams." (In my defense, those dreams I blew up typically involved someone risking an eye, being lit on fire, or even both). The truth is when the rubber hits the road; my boys know that when I pray, I hear from God and what I bring out of the prayer room they honor. God called my bluff when I set out to pray this time. The stipulation I put in that we would all be in agreement was really no match for God's plan for Adam. I threw it out there as a way to stall or, better, cancel Adam's plan. What I needed to understand is this never was Adams' plan. It was God's plan.

If God ordains something for your child, God is going to do it with or without you. But wow! It's so much more fun if you bless their journey along the way. I had full intentions of never agreeing to this preposterous idea of Adam joining the Navy. This way, we would never agree, and he would never be able to go. But God! He has a way of turning hearts towards Him if only you let Him. I was asking God to change the heart of Adam and/or his father, all the while God was actually changing mine. In the end, God answered my prayer about Adam not being able to move unless we were all in agreement. We were all in agreement. It just wasn't the agreement I had thought it would be when I set out to pray. I was trusting and believing that God was moving and doing something now, knowing that I would only come to understand the reason later.

Don't ever allow your own emotions and hang-ups to stop you from giving your children their mother's blessing, a blessing that will drive them straight into the places God is leading them. They need you. It's the most selfless act of love you can do for your children when you surrender them to God's purpose. It is a great act of faith and trust, believing in God's purposes above your own wants, needs, or understanding.

I believe Mary gave us the most remarkable example of a mother's blessing as she stood at the foot of the cross and watched her son be crucified for all mankind. Her baby boy was enduring the most horrific form of suffering and death. With a scene so painful for a mother to witness, I dare say she would have welcomed her own death just to end her pain. Yet, Mary knew, though she could not possibly understand the fullness of it, in that very moment as horrific as it was, that Jesus was surely "about his Father's business." She had to not only *let* him endure it, but she had to *release* him in her heart to endure it. I believe her trust in her son Jesus and her faith in the Father's plan for him was much greater than her need to understand what was happening. After all, she had been trusting God since before He had brought her the news that the Holy Spirit would come upon her and she would bear a son, having never known a man. She had a history with God, and now she was holding tightly onto the truth that God had never failed her yet, even when she never fully understood everything He was doing. Surely, He had a plan now as well. That is, I believe, the only way a mother would have the strength to stand there and witness the horror unfolding before her. Mary, at the foot of the cross - that's the power of a mother's blessing. She was trusting and believing that God was moving and doing something now, knowing she would only come to understand the reason later.

It is also very clear that the mother's blessing Mary was offering to her son did not go unnoticed by Jesus. Even as he hung on the cross suffering and dying, He honored her as His mother. It was during this time that Jesus made sure His mama would be well taken care of after He left. He did this by handing down the charge for John to care for Mary as his own mother. What a powerful moment!

No matter what it looks like or feels like, we can never allow our need to understand be bigger than our faith that God is in control of our lives and the lives of our children. He has a plan.

For the foundations of the earth are the Lord's;

upon them, he has set the world

1 SAMUEL 2:8B

Nothing man can do can change what God is in control of. He has set into motion a plan for your child's life since the foundations of the earth. He is in complete control. He keeps the world spinning on its axis, and He aligns the steps of the righteous. There is nothing He can't do.

THOUGHTS

THOUGHTS

Two

WINGS & ARROWS

I WAS FLIPPING THROUGH A RANDOM CATALOG one day while riding shotgun in the car with my husband. It was a catalog of trinkets and whatnots, all the stuff you don't need because it just collects dust, but it's so fun to look at. In there, I spotted a silver necklace. The charm on the chain was two half-spheres lying one on top of the other that formed a sweet little silver ball charm. When the top half of the sphere was lifted off, you could then see that hidden inside the sphere were little robin-egg-blue beads in a little nest. You had the option to order up to four beads which would represent the "birds" in your "nest." I said to my husband, "OH! I need one of these with two little birds in the nest!" He sweetly replied, "Hunny, we don't have any birds left in our nest, so we will have to get you the empty one." While that stung like a hornet, sadly, he was right.

While raising my boys, somewhere in the back of my mind, I knew this day would come. After all, I had spent many hours teaching them how to become men. How to handle money. How to be great husbands. I had taught them about character and integrity. I had taught them about Jesus. I had told them how I pray that one day they would become godly men and the spiritual heads of their families. I had told them how I have also been praying for their wives since the day they were born. I had been preparing them for leaving from the start. Making them ready to make wise choices. To stand on their own. To fly with great, strong wings. Somehow though, the *reality* of them actually leaving never really came to mind. I never mentally walked through the steps of what that would look like. In all my preparations in getting them ready to fly, I forgot to prepare myself.

In May of 2012, Adam was sworn into the United States Navy at the MEPS Center in Lansing, Michigan. In September of the same year, he left for boot camp. I had been bracing myself for his leave date, knowing that it was going to be hard, but surely it couldn't be much harder than what I had gone through when he left for college. After all, I had already started down the empty nest road. I had already watched my oldest bird fly the nest once. When we left him at the college dorm, I was thinking this was as bad as separation heartache can get. However, I soon found out that the separation the military brings was far worse.

As the leave date loomed closer, it became super clear that this was going to be nothing like sending him off to college. There was never a time I couldn't get to my son. He was always just a phone call or text away. So was I. This was going to be a new sort of separation with no way of me knowing how he was or where he was. The military world was so foreign to me. I didn't have a clue what was in store for either of us. The unknown territory called military did not sound like it was going to be a fun land to cross.

We went through the motions in preparation for his leaving. We had the going away party. We made his favorite foods. We went on the movie date night. We even went on a small family trip. I tried my hardest to stay strong and encouraging. After all, God had just taught me about the mother's blessing. It was now time to walk it out. Not just for him, but for me to get through this, I knew God was going to have to carry it and me.

His last night home, I barely slept. I had lain awake most of the night with all the 'what ifs' and unknowns running through my head. Your mind can be very creative in the still and silent of the night and not always in a good way. Sometimes you take yourself down a dreadful journey that in reality may never come to pass. A scenario will come to mind, and then you spend useless time trying to work out every angle and possibility. Then you come to your senses, you shake it off, and before long, you are at it again with a whole other made-up scenario you waste time and sleep hours trying to solve. That was going on in my mind all night long.

Very early in the morning, when the house was still dark and quiet with sleep, I slipped from my bed, carefully climbed the stairs avoiding all the creaky parts, and crept to Adam's room. I stood in his doorway, listening for any sign that he was awake. There wasn't any. I knew this was another "last time" moment. On tippy-toe, I walked over to where he lay sleeping and carefully crawled onto his queen size bed with him. I just laid there looking at him, watching him sleep, and listening to him breathe. This was my little boy. Others would surely not see it, but there beneath the man that he had become, I could still see my chubby-cheeked toddler. White blonde hair. Bright blue eyes. Wearing his red fireman boots everywhere he went. I smiled through my tears at the memories. How did we get here so fast?

There are not any words in the English language to describe what I was feeling in that moment. All I know is that a mother's heart was never designed to let go, and it felt like mine was being ripped from my chest.

I knew this goodbye was going to stick. This wasn't the same as watching him hop around on the ground, fumbling with his newly grown wings, trying to find his flight at college. This was far different. This time he stood perched, his talons gripping the branch while his wings were spread wide, pumping and ready. It was a sight to see. Absolutely breathtaking! As broken-hearted as I was, I was so excited to see him in flight. The anticipation was great. I could not wait to watch him soar and see where his flight would take him. I was so proud of him!

Children are a heritage from the Lord, offspring a reward from him. Like arrows in the hands of a warrior are children born in one's youth. Blessed is the man whose quiver is full of them. They will not be put to shame when they contend with their opponents in court.

PSALM 127:3-5

This scripture is about children being likened to arrows in the hands of a warrior. Arrows are only put in the hand when the warrior is ready to do something with them. Only when the warrior is ready to launch them. Arrows are meant to fly. They have to be released to fulfill their purpose. The same goes for our children. Only when we can release them into their God-ordained destiny can they fulfill their purpose. The arrows are ready and waiting to be released; it's up to the warrior to release them. While our children are growing up, we are lining up the shot, exhaling slowly, then holding our breath to still our shaking so that we can direct the arrow with precision. Then, when the timing comes, we release it and watch it soar!

I had a dream about this very thing. In the dream, I was working really hard to hone my skills as an archer. I was shooting and shooting and shooting, trying hard to land the arrow where I had intended it to go. I never saw the target in my dream. I don't even know what I was shooting at. It was more about me perfecting the action of release. I do remember being excited in my dream because I was learning. I was getting better with every pull and every release. I also remember in the dream that I had one arm that was completely battered from the strings. In the dream, I showed my battered arm to my husband with a smile on my face. I was more excited that I was getting better at shooting than I was upset that my arm was raw and blistered and black and blue. I looked at the wound proudly as proof of how hard I was trying to perfect my skills. My husband's reply as he looked at my wound in the dream was, "I can help you with your release." And that was the end of my dream.

I didn't think much of it until the next day when I was telling my husband about the dream. When I got to the part of the battered arm, before I had finished the sentence, he was nodding his head yes. I stopped talking mid-sentence and asked, "Why are you nodding?" He said, "That happens when you first start practicing with a bow." Imagine that.

Now, I have only shot a bow once in my life. I was at eighth-grade camp, and archery was one of the field courses. We were handed these rustic longbows with a single string and flimsy little arrows. I was awful at it, and it took far too long even to get the arrow positioned on the string, let alone get one to fly. I was seriously over it before it had started. Well, I pinched my finger so bad between the string and the arrow the first go-round, it drew blood, and I never tried it again. Mad at having been forced to try this idiotic field course to the point of injury, coupled with thirteen-year-old girl drama and secretly just plain embarrassed that I was so horrible at it, I opted out of archery class for the remainder of the week. Later in life, whenever I was around fancier, more modern-day bows, they all belonged to men, and the draw weight on them was so great I was never strong enough to pull it back. Needless to say, I really had no desire to get invested in the sport. So, an archer, I am not.

As it turns out, new archers have a tendency to bang up their arms quite badly while practicing and learning to shoot. I have seen the little gloves consisting of only the three leather fingertips and a wrist strap. These tips cover the fingers used to pull back the string. I imagine after repeated pulls of the string, your fingertips get sore, thus the need for the leather tips. I have also seen the cool leather arm cuffs that archers wear in movies. I was confident they were only for costume sake and reserved for those who truly had mastered the craft and earned the right to wear such amazingly cool things. However, after doing some research, I found out that all this time, they were wearing them as a safety feature and not just to look cool. Who knew they were not only for aesthetics?

The arm holding the bow is held out at full extension in front of you. The string, when it is pulled back and then released from the opposite hand, has the potential to hit and scrape across the fully extended arm as it sends the arrow flying. Depending on the bow, the strings, and the draw weight, those strings can pack a punch. I, however, never stuck with it long enough to have the need for a protective arm sleeve. Can you even imagine how complete my drama-induced melt-down would have been in the eighth grade if I injured an entire arm and not just pinched my finger skin?

I say all this because, in my dream, I was a woman in pursuit of becoming an archer, something I would never pursue in my real life. My pretty badly injured, purple, bruised, and bloodied arm was also included in that dream, again nothing I have ever experienced or even seen on another human. The substance of this dream, along with what my husband had said about the arm, was how I knew God was trying to tell me something. As I sat before the Lord and asked Him what this dream was about, this is what He gave me.

 One way or another, you are going to have to let your arrows - your sons - go. You have to release them. This isn't about the arrows. They will do what they are designed to do. They are made to fly. This isn't about the bow, the means by which they are launched. This is about you—the archer. Right now, you feel banged up, gouged up, bruised up, and battered up because you can't quite figure out the release. You don't trust the bow to do its job, so you are trying to control it. You fight the bow, no matter how it batters you because you don't trust it. You don't trust Me; I am the means by which your arrows - your boys - will be launched. You aren't hurting the arrows. You aren't hurting the bow. You are hurting yourself. I see the tenacity of your heart to get it right, but you are doing it of your own might and strength, and you're doing it your own way. If you keep at it, your arm will forever stay wounded. But, if you let me show you, I can help you with your release. Trust me. It's time to let them fly.

Mothers, since the dawn of time, have been watching their children leave home. I honestly couldn't believe I struggled so much with something that should be so natural. After all, we didn't raise them to stay at home for the rest of their lives. We raised them to go! To live successful lives! Realizing our children are ready to leave home, yet having it be the thing we dread the most is the juxtapose of motherhood. Them being ready to leave at some level is our own fault. It means we have done something right! My heart needed to be handed up to the Lord, and I needed to trust Him to bring me into the next season of my life and my family's life. If letting them go was easy, I don't think God would have found it necessary to include the instructional passage in the very first book of the Bible:

A man will leave his father and mother

GENESIS 2:24

God knew this was going to be tough for us. He thought of this before we ever got here and gave us a nod in this scripture. I can see Him smiling kindly and nodding His head at me, saying, "This is for his good. It's time for you to release him." In order to walk in God's fullness for our lives and for them to walk in theirs, we have to let them go. It's by God's design they leave even when it feels like we don't have it within us to let them go, even when we may not like where they are going.

When my grandfather and father entered the military, they had no choice as they were called up by the draft during times of war and conflict. When I was in high school, and the boys I graduated with were choosing to enlist, it was because they either had no other options or they had nowhere else to go. Dysfunctional family life made them realize that Uncle

Sam may be the most reliable relative they had at the time. It is through this distorted lens that I originally viewed joining the military. When my boys came to me with these crazy ideas of signing up, I had to make sure they were not doing it because they felt they had no other choice. Military, to me, was the last resort. You'd only go if you absolutely had nowhere else to go. My children had places to go. They had options. They had both started colleges to become anything they wanted. We would help them get there. If they didn't want college, they could apprentice through our family business and get their license in the trades, a fading industry in great demand. I had built all sorts of dreams and aspirations for my children. We had tossed around all the ways they could build their lives while they were growing up and throughout their high school years. None of the ways I had thought of included the military uniform. Interestingly enough, the military wasn't either one of their first choices either. It came after a season of walking with the Lord and trying to find their way.

As I was studying about the archer, there was something to note about the arrows. The most common reason for shots being consistently off-target is that the arrows are too weak or not strong enough for the bow weight, which causes them to bend too much in flight, making them hit off the desired mark. Does this feel like an AH-HA moment to anybody else but me? God couldn't shoot them to the target of the military until they were strong enough to go! So, if this feels like you have been clobbered out of the blue with this idea of the military coming from your children, re-member it is not out of the blue for God. He's been doing a work in them, getting them strong enough for this very target.

When I drive through cities and towns, even backcountry roads, and

I see something being torn down or falling down, my heart breaks a little. Buildings on a town square that once held a mom-and-pop mercantile full of goods and friendly faces and a heart for the community, now being imploded to make room for some nationwide commercial franchise that looks like all the others, having no pulse of the people in that community. Old farmhouses that hold generations of memories and happiness, hardship and grit, being pulled down to make room for wind turbines or subdivisions. I imagine the families that once dwelt in those homes. The babies born there. The weddings. The holidays. I imagine the young couples that started small businesses in those old mom-and-pop storefronts. The dreams, the passion, the risk, the unknown. And for a moment in their lives, wasn't it the greatest time of all? The excitement. The possibility. The start of something amazing beginning to come to life. Now to see that dream being torn down, well, my heart gets sad. Maybe it's because I have lived in the same house for the past thirty years. My husband began building that home when he was just nineteen years old. It's where we moved in the day after our wedding. It's where we brought our sons home when they were born. There is a wooden beam where my husband carved out "I {heart} You" as a wedding gift to me. A declaration of his love for me permanently etched into our home. There is a grow wall where I have marked the growth of my boys since the day they could stand against it. There are feathers all over this nest that reflect a life lived. It holds all the memories of every day of my amazing adult life, and I cannot ever imagine someone tearing it down. It could also be that I relate as a small business owner. My husband and I started with nothing but a truck and some tools. I know what it is to risk everything to start and grow a business from the ground up in hopes of providing for your family. I know the strength and courage it takes. I realize I am probably more sentimental than most, but when we drive past those places being torn down or in ruins, I always say, "That was someone's dream," and I lament a bit as we drive past.

One day as I was doing this lamenting while I looked out the passenger seat window at a building I saw going up, in the place where someone's "dream" once stood, God spoke to my sad little heart.

" *Sometimes, Sherry, I have to tear something down before I can build something new.*

I knew He wasn't just talking about this building I was looking at. He was talking about the things I had built up in my own heart. Things *I* had built, not things He had built. Things *I* had wanted, not things He wanted for me. Things *I* was hanging on to, not things He had meant for me to hold. Ultimately, He was referring to anything I was hanging on to tighter than I was hanging onto Him. Those things are referred to as idols. Anything that is exalted in my life higher than God is an idol. Idols can take many forms. They can be as bold as a statue of a god or goddess like the Asherah Poles in the Old Testament or as subtle as putting greater trust in my own ability and talents over that of God. Both the Old and New Testaments warn us to tear these idols down.

He (King Hezekiah) did what was right in the eyes of the Lord, just as his father David had done. He removed the high places, smashed the sacred stones, and cut down the Asherah poles.

2 KINGS 18:3-4

"

Sometimes
I have to
tear something down
before
I can build
something new.

———————

Now, the idol worship at the time of Hezekiah's rule was pretty extreme. The people were burning their own children as sacrifices to their gods. They had set up altars in high places, carved and planted trees known as Asherah poles, and stacked sacred stones as places of worship to these false gods. Hezekiah was just one of many who smashed and tore down the high places. Asa, Josiah, Jehoshaphat, and Gideon are other men of God who tried to eradicate this false worship and point the people back to God.

I think it is pretty safe to say, these are probably not the idols most of us are dealing with today, but the next passage might ring a little closer to home.

We demolish arguments and every pretension that sets itself up against the knowledge of God, and we take captive every thought to make it obedient to Christ.

2 CORINTHIANS 10:5

In the Greek lexicon, it will read like this: We pull down reasoning and thought, and every height which is lifted up against the knowledge, doctrine, wisdom, and understanding way of God. This passage tells us that it doesn't have to be a physical pile of rocks or a statue for it to be an idol. Our thoughts can actually be an idol set in the high places of our lives. Wrong thinking, wrong believing, or anything that pulls our focus away from God, out of His presence, and into the center of our self-made high place, is an idol.

Hanging onto selfish dreams for my sons or for myself *through* my sons was a high place God wanted to tear down in my life so that He could rebuild in *me* something new and fulfill in *them* His plan. Part of the dream God had for me was hinged on the dreams He had for my sons. If I continued to hold onto my self-made dreams for *them*, He could never complete the dream He had for me. My dreams for them didn't include the military for many reasons, but the one reason it should *become* my dream that it *needs* to become my dream is that it is God's dream.

This is often easier said than done. What if God tells you to do something terrible? Something impossible to fathom? Like, put your baby in a basket, seal the basket with pine pitch and send it down the Nile? If that baby doesn't drown, it is surely going to get eaten by the anaconda and crocodiles. It's a horrible idea. There is no way a mother is going to do that! Yet, horrible as that might sound, if she hadn't done it, there could have been a whole people group that never got out of slavery in Egypt. There may never have been a parted Red Sea. There may never have been the stone tablets etched with the Ten Commandments. All the pages and chapters in our Bible would look a whole lot scanter without the testament Moses, who was not only kept safe in that basket but for whom God made an almost unbelievable provision. Only God could have managed to have Moses' own mother hired to nurse and care for her own infant son, and that was just the start of seeing the hand of God raise him up to do amazing things.

On the front end, some of the stories and events we read in the Bible sound like terrible ideas. Horrible things. Really, really bad plans. Things we would stop if we could. Esther being forced into the palace. Moses being floated down the river. David going up against Goliath. Jesus- God in the flesh, being crucified. All of these things, I would have stopped if

I could have, but look at what I would have prevented had I been able to. There are all these very large pieces of God's Kingdom being moved around and aligned, and they have been doing that since God first spoke the earth into existence. We are all part of that big design. Our Kingdom destiny is set by His hand to collide with earthly happenings to bring Heaven down, "on earth as it is in heaven." As we keep reading through the Bible and we get to the end of the stories, we get to see what God accomplished when His elect walked in His dream and destiny for them. On the back end of these stories and events, we see God move. We see just how awesome our God is and how each of these people advanced, not because they had it all together, not because they thought they could do it on their own, but because they trusted Him to do it through them. Just like Mordecai says to Esther right before she goes to do the very thing she was destined to do. Remember, she has no idea this is her destiny. She does not yet know just how big God is going to use her for His Kingdom; this is the front end of the story.

"Who knows but that you have come to your royal position for such a time as this?"

ESTHER 4:14

Who knows, ladies, what your children have come into this position for? But won't it be amazing to watch it unfold in God's hands? And not just what they have come into the position for, but what *you* have come into this position for as well. Just wait until you see the back end of God's ultimate plan that you may feel right now is a really bad idea on the front end.

My sons hitting their target of military has led me to see not only a new dream God had for them but also the new dreams God had for me. I now have a beat in my heart to be a watchman on the wall for our military and our country. I am able to raise awareness and give insight to others about a world that many never get to see. I am able to pray with and for other moms who are watching their children sign up to go and fight for this nation and the freedoms it provides. I am able to pen these very words to other moms and bring them along on this journey with me. None of this would ever have happened had I not let God tear down my self-made plans and dreams for my sons. Now I am running with perseverance the new race He has marked out for me. If there is one thing that has killed my know-it-all perspective, it's coming to terms with God is God, and He knows what He's doing far more than I do. It's best I let Him lead.

It may be time for us as moms to recalibrate our dreams. It's time to ask God, " Are You breaking down the high things in my life to build something new in me?" The bottom line is whether it's a little bird now grown and ready to leave the nest or an arrow in the hand of a warrior, the destiny is the same; they are created to soar. We have to let them go. We have to release them into their destiny no matter how ridiculous or horrible it looks at the onset. Whatever it is that is preventing us from doing that, we need to let God tear it down so that He can build something new. Something He always meant for us to have. If it's God's plan, I want it. If it's not, then it's a high place, and that has got to go.

Take some time with the Lord to journal your thoughts on learning to release your children. It is a process. Be gentle with yourselves. Let God speak to your heart. He is talking, and He is leading. You just have to listen.

THOUGHTS

THOUGHTS

Three

LOSS & FOUND

IN THE AGE OF TECHNOLOGY and smartphones, it is almost impossible not to have some kind of a pulse on where your kids are and what they are doing at any given time. This has greatly enabled us as parents to keep track of our sons and daughters far easier than it was for our parents. I often think about when I was a teen and how my parents did not have the luxury of knowing where we were or even have the ability to reach us. I can't imagine not having the ability to contact my kids in my pocket at all times. So, when the child you've had a constant connection with since birth suddenly goes off-grid, it's a shock to the system. The silence is probably the hardest thing. The not knowing. When we don't know and are left to wonder, our minds can run away with us. Being inside your own head and alone with thoughts is not always the best place to be.

When Adam left for boot camp, it was about three weeks before we received the first letter from him. During that time, I'll be honest. I was a wreck. I was up all night. I wasn't eating. I'd start crying at the drop of a hat. I was just plain miserable. There were several nights when my husband would wake to find my side of the bed empty. He would stumble out of our bedroom, all sleepy-eyed, and find me sitting somewhere in the dark crying. Praying. Sulking. The defeat and helplessness would show on his face. He had no way of knowing how to help bring me back. I just could not find my way out of this place. It was dark. It was out of my control. I hated it. I also really felt alone and isolated. No one around me could understand what I was going through or help me battle through it. Instead of trying to explain myself to others, I found it easier to just pull back into seclusion. I didn't need people making me feel worse about how I was feeling by trying to fix it or help me toughen up. I really didn't even want to toughen up. Part of me thought that if I didn't hurt so much, I would feel nothing at all. Being numb seemed worse than the misery I was currently in, so I was choosing to stay in misery, embracing the pain that came with it.

The dark blanket I was personally wrapped in shielded me from the toll this was taking on my family. My husband and my youngest son were also sorting through this new season. They, too, had a son and a brother in the military and no longer home. They, too, hated the silence. They, too, were navigating through this in their own way. But through my clouded lens, this seemed so much harder for me.

Our youngest son Matthew was a junior in high school when our oldest son left for the Navy. He was on the football team. He loved it so much, and the team was doing amazing. For the first time in many years, the Shelby Tigers were not only winning games, but they made it into the semifinals for the state championship. There was so much to be excited about. The whole town was jumping with excitement. On Friday nights, we would head out to watch his games. We were so proud of him. He'd run out onto the field, scan the stands searching for our faces, and when finding us, he would always reach out his hand and point in our direction. I'd beat my fist on my heart twice and then throw my pointing hand back in his direction. It was my way of saying all the things in my heart for him without having to actually say them. "We got you, kiddo! We are right here!"

Then just like clockwork, that electric excitement of the game would be cloaked in a dark blanket as the flag was raised and the National Anthem played. There I was, struggling to get the lyrics out between sobbing gulps. The flag and the National Anthem mean something more when your son is defending them. It was closer to home at the football games. I was raw.

I had lost my joy. I could not find my feet. I am not normally a depressed person. I rarely find myself down in the dumps. On a scale of one to ten, one being comatose and ten being so excited you literally explode; I normally sit between a seven and an eight. Everyday. That is my default personality. But here I was at what I felt was a two or, at best, a three. It was such a hard time for me.

One day after weeks of this, Matthew came to me with my favorite cookies, chocolates, and a greeting card. It wasn't my birthday. It wasn't a holiday. It was just because. I was thinking to myself, "What a sweet boy!" as he handed me the gifts and card. I gave him a hug, humbled by his thoughtfulness. Then my reaction quickly changed to feelings and thoughts of "my poor son, what have I done?" When I opened the envelope and pulled out the card, the air completely left my lungs. I was undone and without any words. When had this gotten so bad? The outside of the card read, "So sorry for your loss." In my hands, I held a sympathy card. It was a sympathy card for the loss of Adam!

Matthews' thoughtfulness was absolutely beautiful and so incredibly heartbreaking at the same time. My 17-year-old son saw something I hadn't seen myself. I was grieving. I was grieving the loss of my oldest son and hurting my youngest son as I did it. Up until that moment, I had no idea that this was grief. I knew it was something, but grief never crossed my mind. Sad? Yes. Lost? You bet. Confused? Absolutely. Helpless and out of my control? Yes, and yes. But grief? That never crossed my mind. It took what I believe was the prompting of the Holy Spirit to lead my son to the store to buy this card for me, for me to see what was happening. Reading this card, my eyes were wide open to what I was actually feeling and going through. Grief.

Once I realized that grief was the name of that dark blanket that kept showing up, I immediately moved into defiance mode. I needed to get rid of this thing. I had to quit grieving. I had no right to grieve! My son wasn't dead, for goodness sakes; he had just joined the military. How silly of me to be grieving someone who is still alive. I told myself to knock it off. How dare I believe, for even a moment, that I deserve the right to feel an emotion that is exclusively reserved for losing a loved one to death? This is nothing like death. Get a grip! I was embarrassed to admit what I was feeling. I was ashamed. Appalled. I hated myself for it. Kids from all over the nation are in boot camp right now, and I was sure no other mother was acting so abhorrently. For. The. Love. Stop it. Surely, if I had enough of these talks with myself, I would snap out of the madness. This was my game plan of getting myself through the grief. I wasn't tolerating it. Not for a moment.

Within a matter of days after this revelation, I was visiting with a dear friend. She had just lost her husband. She noticed that I had not been myself of late and asked how I was doing with Adam being gone. I instantly wanted to change the subject. Here she was, newly widowed, and she was asking *me* how *I* was doing. What kind of horrible friend was I? I was supposed to comfort her! Not the other way around. She is a godly woman, and seeing me trying to dodge the question, she pressed in. Then, suddenly and uncontrollably, the dam broke, and I began to share my heart with her. When I say "share my heart," I really mean that I let every last drop of pent-up emotion I was holding in come crashing down on her. I told her how I realized that I was in a stage of grief over my son, *who is still alive,* and how ashamed I was. I told her I had no right to grieve, and I had no right to lay this on her. *Especially* not on her, the one fully entitled to that emotion. I apologized over and over through my gulps and sobs. I couldn't even look at her.

After I was done falling apart, my sweet friend smiled and grabbed my hand. She explained to me that grief is grief, and we don't get to pick when it comes, how it comes, or why it comes. She told me that grief is a cruel thing to walk through. It can and will show its head at the most unexpected, inconvenient times, and we have no control over it. She validated everything I was going through. She spoke life and truth into the part of me that needed it so desperately. Then she did something amazing. This friend, who was mourning the loss of her own husband, gave me permission to grieve. It was like this huge weight had been lifted. The grieving I had been trying to kill or make go away by avoidance and sheer bullheadedness and defiance she allowed me to accept in myself. She told me that unless I let myself go through the grief, it will never go away.

What I took away from that time with my sweet friend and the times spent since with the Lord is this. If your heart is feeling a loss of any kind, you can pretty much count on grief to follow. And just as the losses are not all the same, our grief will not be all the same. Therefore, we cannot compare our grief with the grief of others as it is never going to be or look the

"

grief is grief,

and we don't get to pick

when it comes,

how it comes,

or why it comes.

We have to walk through it.

_____

same. We also don't get to choose when it comes, and we cannot just will it to be gone. We have to walk through it. This was step two.

Once I gave myself permission to grieve, the second thing I had to get a grip on was getting *through* the grieving process. I had had no idea up to this point how the dark place I was in was affecting Matthew and Mike. I guess I thought I was hiding it better than I was and was quietly suffering alone. It hadn't even occurred to me how my actions were hurting the ones at home. My heart was sad about Adam, but when Matthew handed me that card, my heart encountered a second fracture. My little boy was watching his mother come undone at the seams, and all he could think to do to make it better was love his broken mama back to good. He was going to do it by any means he had, which included showering me with the things he knew I loved in hopes he'd see my smile return. So I had to get through this for all of us, especially Matthew. He needed his mom back. When I knew it was grief, I also knew that for us to be a healthy family, I had to find my feet. I had to let God heal me. I looked around at the pieces of myself scattered about, completely lost, and I watched as God put me back together. In Him, I was once again found.

I don't really know how long it took, and I don't remember a time that I just snapped out of it. However, I did come out of it. After I received that sympathy card, I spent the next while praying for the healing balm of Gilead to wash over my raw, broken wounds of loss. The scripture I clung to then and so many times since is this:

But we have this treasure in jars of clay, to show that this all-surpassing power is from God and not from us. We are pressed on every side, but not crushed; perplexed, but not in despair; persecuted, but not abandoned; struck down, but not destroyed.

2 CORINTHIANS 4:7-9

I said this verse over and over and over. At times when I felt like the feelings of loss were too much to bear, and I could not get up because the weight of it was too great, I would read and recite this verse. I posted it on my bathroom mirror, and I pinned it up above my desk at work. Getting me through this was not too big for God, and I would rise from these ashes. Not only would I rise, but I would be stronger because of it. After all, He had set my feet in this place. There must be a reason why. I had to let Him heal my heart and bring me to the why.

Adam's letters eventually found their way to us, and they came in the mail once a week. He had a small chunk of time on Sundays where he could write his letters. They were full of tidbits of his time at basic training. Some made me mad as a hornet, and some made me laugh until I had tears. Some made me cry with joy over the favor and blessing and victories of God in Adam's life. Some of the letters made me want to rescue him. All of them made me anxious to get my hands on him when he finally graduated.

All through the eight weeks of Adam's basic training, I was reaching into the Throne room of God to guide and heal me through this time of sorrow. What I found was that God was not only with me holding me up; he was bandaging me, supporting my weight as I walked, and providing sustenance to my soul as I limped along. I had a goal of healing, no matter how hard it seemed, and because of the tender, unrelenting care and love

He had for me, He wasn't going to let me quit. He was feeling my pain, hearing my prayers, listening to my cries, and even gathering my tears.

Record my lament; put my tears in your wineskin,
are they not in your record?

PSALM 56:8

The King James translation of this verse uses the words "a bottle" instead of "wineskin." A tear bottle or a lachrymatory is used to catch the tears of those who mourn. This is a tradition that goes back 3,000 years. In Psalm 56:8, David is referring to the belief that God keeps a record of our deepest sorrows and holds our tears in *His* bottle. We do not have to collect them in our own bottles because every tear we shed is precious to Him, and He longs to carry that pain for us. Tears are a language God understands. We don't have to validate them. We don't need to explain them. Sometimes we *can't* explain them. All we know is there is a pain so deep that only tears can wash the pain away. As we pour out our brokenness in tears, He collects those tears and holds them dearly. This is how deeply He hurts when we hurt.

Also, His care for us in our earthly pain is just a glimpse of what is to come one day when we see Him face to face.

He will wipe every tear from their eyes. There will be
no more death or mourning or crying or pain,
for the old order of things has passed away.

REVELATION 21:4

When we see Him face to face, there will be a moment where again we will have no words, and our tears will speak for us one last time. Then, instead of collecting our broken hearts to Himself in the form of tears in His bottle, He will wipe our tears clean away. Never again will we feel grief, or sorrow, or pain. Ladies! There will come a day. Until then, we press on.

Ebb and flow are words used to describe the tide of the ocean. The ebb is the outgoing of the waves as they pull back into the sea, and the tide drains from the shore. The flow is the water rising with the incoming waves as they come racing back, crashing onto the shore. It's a rhythmical pattern of the coming of rushing water and retreat of it returning to the sea. Just like in the sea, there is an ebb and flow in the military world. Just as you have accepted and maybe even embraced an area of this life and are standing in the ebb, there seems to be another sucker punch, another flow, waiting in the wings. It can be brutal. Our resilience to stay the course is having a hope that does not disappoint - hope in Jesus Christ. I know that I know I was fashioned, equipped, and born to be a military mom because this is where I find myself. I don't know why. I don't always feel like I have what it takes for this position. I don't always feel equipped or strong enough. What I do know is that God doesn't set us in places to fail. God never fails. It's up to me to lean into Him and to get the Kingdom goods to succeed. There are strengths in this calling I have yet to tap into and anointings I have yet to find. As I walk this road, I draw on my truth in Him to keep me resilient, and then I can be the strength my sons need me to be. That's how we survive the ebb and flow of the military. It hits us hard and knocks us down with its relentless flow, but as we hang on to the Father's hand, He will snatch us back up to our rightful standing. It's our resilience to get back up, to reclaim the fight, to ready ourselves, and to tell the flow that it doesn't win that we will find ourselves standing in the ebb. We've experienced the times of God holding us up, we've been steadfast in those times of flow, and we have a testimony of how we've stood as victors in the ebb. That testimony, which is recounting of God's goodness, gets us stronger and able to withstand the flows that will follow.

Once I found myself sure-footed and standing in the ebb after the knock-down flow of boot camp, it was only a matter of time until the cycle started all over again. One of the gifts God gave us is that Adam would be graduating during the Thanksgiving holiday. What typically happens is that after the graduation, families get to have the one day of graduation with their son or daughter, and the very next day, the Sailors get flown out to their A school, wherever that may be. With Adam graduating on Wednesday and Thanksgiving Day being a holiday, we had Wednesday and all of Thanksgiving Day with him before he flew out to his A school on Friday. In preparation for this celebration, I had made an entire homemade turkey dinner. I packed the whole thing up in the car and brought it with us as I was determined to get that boy some home cooking before he flew off to the next place. I was in the ebb of military mom life. The yuck was on its way out. I had found my way and withstood the first incoming flow, and I was certainly at this point standing in the ebb!

We drove to Chicago on Tuesday. It was dark as we came into the city. All of us were excited that we were finally going to see him. I felt like my feet would never touch the ground again. I was so happy. The wait was over. I was about to get my hands on my boy! As I was looking out at the promising bright city lights of the Chicago skyline, my cell phone rang. It was Adam! "Are you guys here?" He was just as excited and anxious as we were. I assured him we were almost to our hotel, and wild horses wouldn't keep us from getting to him the next day.

We talked about the graduation logistics for a bit, and also about dinner at the hotel after, and then he asked, "Can I talk to Matt?" There it was. That pit in my stomach. Something in his voice triggered my mama's senses.

I passed the phone to Matthew in the back seat. He talked quietly for a few minutes, and then the phone got passed to Mike, who was driving. Now I was certain something was afoot. It was something they were all preparing for, something they were dreading having to tell me. They had done this in the past. All of them coming together to form this protective shield around me at times when they knew I would be falling in or out of my pretty stable range between a 7-8 on the emotional scale. If it was going to cause mom to fall off the bottom of the scale or explode off the top, they called in reinforcements. When Mike ended the phone call, there was silence from both of them. The excitement that was in the car just moments before was completely sucked out. The energy shifted in just a few short moments. I knew I had to ask. I knew I needed to know, even if it was bad. Here comes the flow.

I don't remember who told me if it was Mike or Matthew, but I remember hearing "Adam is being stationed in Japan." I knew this meant that once he went through a few short weeks of A school, he would be immediately sent to Japan for a four-year contract. Four years. I remember looking out at the city again, and this time the lights didn't look so promising. They didn't look as bright. Instead, it was just one warbled light mixed with the dark of the sky as I looked out through my tears. Quietly, I let this sink in. Quietly, I prayed. Japan is so far away. I knew that this would be another bruise on my mama heart. I also knew that God had led me through this military grief once before. He had given me clarity. He had given me tools. He had brought me hope and strength to stay the course. He held me up during the first flow. I knew we'd find our way through this too. I was hopeful the dark I found myself in the first go-round would be flooded with His light this second time around. My son was going to Japan. This was a flow for him as well. He needed us to be praying him through. I had a Kingdom job before me. I was not going to turn back now. I'd find the strength. I would stay standing as I faced this flow as it came at me with a force so great it meant to knock me down, but first, I was going to enjoy this ebb, hug my boy, and have a fantastic Thanksgiving dinner before he left.

I learned to let myself feel the feelings and go through the hurt, and I watched Him collect tears from me and replace them with His comfort and strength. As He was scooping up the tears, I learned that if I could praise and thank Him in that place of brokenness, the healing would come much sooner. God, Himself also knows the pain of letting go of a Son for a much greater cause, in a most unimaginable way. The surrender of His Son was so much greater than my surrender. How could I not trust Him to get me through something He knows so much more about than I ever could? I learned to expose that broken place, and right in the midst of my greatest pain, I began to thank Him. "God thank you, for letting me know a love so great it actually feels like it will tear the heart from my chest." There are some that will never know the blessing of a love that great, and I never want to take for granted that I have lived a life with that much love.

When I returned that brokenness to Him and when I exposed it and lifted it up, the praise and thankfulness I chose to put in its place chased away the darkness the enemy wanted to keep me wrapped up in.

Find the praise in your brokenness. Nothing chases away the devil, like the exaltation of the goodness of God. The ebb and flow of military life for the mamas at home will not stop until your child is holding his or her DD-214. While our sons and daughters are serving our country, we need to get stronger. We will find our way through this together. Know that I am praying for you and for your sons and daughters. You are not in this alone. I also need you praying for my sons and for me. I need you on the wall with me. I need you to find that His mercies are new every morning. If today looks grim, remember that tomorrow comes the dawn. Tomorrow there is hope. Tomorrow there are new mercies. Today may feel really hard to get through, but He is with you. WE are with you. Tomorrow.....we ride!

Military life isn't for wimps. It takes a grit most will never know or experience. If you find yourself in a place of grief on this journey, I want you to know you are not alone. I, too, have shared your broken heart in the release of your children into this crazy ebb and flow military life. Endless other moms have experienced it too. Grief also isn't new. People have been going through it since the dawn of time. Let yourself go through it. If you are like me in the beginning and refuse to do it, you will not heal, and that wound will continue to affect you, your husband, and your children. You will stay sunk in the flow of that wave, unable to move or breathe. I am giving you permission to let yourself recognize that this is a loss. There may be people who think you are silly, overreacting, or just plain being a baby. Trust me, I've experienced it, along with all the rude comments that come along with it. I have learned to offer only grace in return. Those who have never walked in my shoes cannot fathom what it is like. They have never been down this road. It's not their fault. Looking from the outside in, they cannot see the strength it takes to release your child into the hands of Uncle Sam. God knows your heart. He knows how hard this is for you. He sees you. He sees your circumstances. As hard as this may be in this moment, this will not destroy you. Get up! Remember whose hand you are holding onto. He will never let go. I still carry that sympathy card in my Bible along with all the other pieces and bits and photos that remind me of His goodness and faithfulness. I never want to forget all He has brought me through. He will get you through this too, and you will come out not only a victor but equipped, stronger, and more sure-footed, ready for the next ebb and flow. You may feel a loss right nows, but believe me when I say you are on the verge of finding all that is to be found!

THOUGHTS

four

BOOTS & HORSES

WHEN I BECAME A MILITARY MOM the second time, the steps of our youngest son looked a whole lot like the steps of our oldest son when each one started out, except they were so very different. Matthew had graduated high school and, like his older brother, decided he would give college a whirl. He moved into a house an hour away from home with several other boys he had played high school football with. Going into it, this seemed like this was going to be a great time of living his best life and finding where he would go next.

However, in a short amount of time, it was clear things were not going well. Unlike his brother deciding to just change things up with his career, things were getting hard for Matthew. He was completely unhappy, and we could tell he was battling something within himself. He was in a terrible headspace, and we were truly concerned about him. School at this time in his life was just not a good fit. He was really struggling. We decided it was best to let him take the next semester off, come home, work for our family business, and regroup. Somewhere in *my* heart, however, I knew what was brewing in his.

From the time he was seven years old, I knew this moment was coming as much as I pushed it down and tried denying it. When he was in the first grade, they had a fill-in-the-blank paper that came home with him. They were to fill in the space provided with "What I Want To Be When I Grow Up." It wasn't a doctor, or a fireman, or even a race car driver. In the mind of a seven-year-old, there are no barriers or reasons to doubt that whatever you choose at that moment would one day come to pass. At an age when you truly believe you can be anything you want to be, my little boy chose a soldier. Now, had it just been that one paper he had written in class at seven years old, I would have smiled at how adorable it was and cast it off as another one of the many cute things my little boy had said. But from that point on, he never really stopped believing that is what he was going to be in some form or another. He mentioned it in passing all the while he was growing up. He loved all things army. All things camo. One Christmas, a ghillie suit was even on his list. Always in the back of my mind was *what if?* What if he really *does* grow up to be a soldier?

There was also something else. Something very important and profound I had been pondering in my heart since before he was born. It was a word spoken over him while I was still pregnant. I was at a women's retreat, and there was a lady there who moves in the prophetic. This amazing woman of God asked if she could pray for my baby and me. Of course! There was no way I would turn down prayer. As she laid her hands on my belly, she said these words, "I see this child's feet on many foreign soils." Wow! What a powerful word! Right then and there, I began to praise God because this could only mean one thing! My baby was going to be a missionary. WooHoo! A prophetic word over your baby doesn't get much better than that. My unborn child was already being prophetically set up to be part of the Great Commission! I left there super excited for his future. I mean, what a great word. I was also over the moon because at the time she gave the word to me, the service was being recorded. I had paid for a cassette tape copy so that I could listen to it over and over. It was a good word!

Looking back, though, I realize I was completely clueless. I imagine God shaking his head and smiling down on me and thinking, "She's close. She's on to something, but she is going to be blown away by what his missions' field will look like." It wasn't until Matthew struggled so hard that first semester of college that I began to sift that prophetic word in my heart. Maybe his wanting to become a soldier for most of his life and the "boots on foreign soil" prophetic word that I'd been pondering all these years go hand in hand. It was as if a light was slowly beginning to turn on as God illuminated that word in my heart. I was taken back to the very moment I heard that word, and I was undone by His thoughtfulness and goodness and love for me and for my son. God had given a Word for my son to a lady I had never met. Then He positioned us both in the same place where my path would have a heavenly collision with hers, and she could breathe that word into the heart and spirit of this young twenty-two-year-old mama. He gave that to me *then* to ponder in my heart in order to prepare and ready me for something that wouldn't take place until nineteen years later! That's how awesome our God is!

Matthew's time at home regrouping from college started in December when winter break began. Within a few weeks, he had found his feet and knew what he wanted to do. In January 2015, as I was riding shotgun in his truck, he laid his hand on mine and, while mustering his courage to broach the subject, softly said, "Mom, I want to go talk to a recruiter." I can tell you the exact spot where we were on US 10 Highway when he said these words.

It is seared in my mind because it's one of those moments I knew would change the entire course of my son's life. I was not surprised. Not even a little. I had actually been expecting this conversation. I had been steeling myself so that I could be ready to respond the way God would have me respond. I had been praying that I would be ready and unshaken and the mother he needed me to be. I had just been waiting for him to settle it for himself and for God's timing to direct him. I knew once he left school, it was only a matter of time before he worked it out with God and in his own heart. Here it was, the time had come, and he was running full speed ahead.

The very next day, we drove down to the recruiter's office. We were led in and asked to sit down at a desk opposite a recruiter. He and Matthew began to talk. I just listened as the recruiter hashed out what his options were. The timelines. The this. The that. The military lingo that I still wasn't great at, especially because we were switching branches of the military, and heaven forbid they should all just use the same lingo to simplify things. But I digress. I just sat silently and listened. I knew this was only the pre-liminary meeting. I had been through this before, and I knew they were only going to cover the basic questions and answers here today. I would listen more closely down the road when this got a little more serious. The recruiter started listing off the job options available to Matthew, and as he listed them one after the other, suddenly, with one of these options, I was snapped back into the fullness of the conversation. It was an experience likened to being in a large crowd with chatter going on all around you, and suddenly someone says your name. Hearing your name spoken somehow carries out among all the voices, and it pulls you to attention. You immedi-ately stop whatever you are doing, saying, or listening to and search out the source of where your name was just spoken. That happened when he spoke this word. This just got serious y'all. As soon as that word came out of that recruiter's mouth, I knew it was *exactly* where Matthew was going. That's the one. That's it! It's like a bell of confirmation rang in my spirit, and I knew this was what his prophetic boots were supposed to be doing. That's what God had been saying to me all this time. I could flashback to moments in this child's life that I didn't realize until that moment there in the recruiter's office made perfect sense for where he was going! I didn't say anything when the recruiter was talking or when I heard that option spoken. I just waited to let God confirm it through Matthew. I knew that if this was God-breathed, Matthew too would have that same ringing bell in his spirit. He did. When that option was put on the table, everything else faded away, and this became the next open door on his journey with the Lord.

Just when you think you have fought and clawed your way to being as strong as you can possibly get, something like this shows up, and you realize you aren't even close. There is a whole new level of strong you know nothing about, and all you can do is grab ahold of God and let Him get you to that new level. Without Him, I knew I wouldn't be able to withstand what was coming. All I could do was tell myself to breathe and not lose it at the recruiter's office. I cannot, due to OPSEC (Operational Security), tell you what that job is because as I am writing this book, he is still on active duty and still in this line of work. What I *can* tell you is that this job puts him directly in harm's way and is an attachment to Special Forces. What I can also tell you is I would be lying if I didn't admit to you that right then and there, I asked God for a different pair of prophetic boots for my son. I mean, come on! I think my literal words to the Lord were, "Really God? You've got to be kidding me!"

As we left the recruiter's office, Matthew was happier than I had seen him in months. He had found his thing. He knew where he was going. He had found his way. I, on the other hand, was completely annoyed. Not only did I have my oldest son serving in the United States Navy stationed in Japan for four years, deployed on an aircraft carrier with an F-18 fighter squadron, working on the flight deck 20 stories above the water (With no safety railing, I might add, which would have made me feel at least a bit better. I joke *but, yikes!! 20 stories!!*), launching and catching fighter jets all while dodging jet fire, and whirling propellers, now God was bringing me THIS? Annoyed is probably not the word.

The only positive thing I had to hold onto was knowing that the military tends to move slowly. With Adam, there were the four months from the time he signed until the time he left for me to get my head around it. We had time. Time for me to ready my heart. Time to gain the strength I knew I'd need. Matthew hadn't even signed yet. That contract wasn't yet available. What he would be signing on for required an open slot for him to enter that specific program. That had to equal even *more* time. Right? If you said 'yes' to that, as I did, you'd be wrong.

The very next day at a restaurant, as Mike, Matthew, and I sat eating lunch, Matthew's phone rang. Do you know how you sometimes have this thing in the pit of your stomach? When your mama senses are trying to tell you something? An intuition that moms sometimes get? That is exactly what I had going on when Matthew's phone went off. It was the same feeling I had in the car right before I was told Adam would be stationed in Japan. When Matthew answered that incoming phone call, he sat stone-still, listening intently to whoever was on the other end. Then, he turned and looked me straight in the eyes as he said into the phone, "I'll call you right back." and hung up. I'm going to be honest. I felt like I was going to throw up. I laid my forehead straight down on that table right in the middle of that restaurant because this was going to take all I had.

Another difference this time around was that Matthew knew how being part of a military family felt. He had been through the changes that took place in our family when Adam left for the Navy. It was a hard adjustment for all of us. Matthew has gone through his own stages of loss and grief. Those boys were best friends. They had been stuck together like glue before Adam left. I love that about my boys. Their bond always makes me smile. Having had to watch Matthew navigate his last two years of high school with his brother being stationed overseas was tough. Missing out on all the incredible moments and memories was as hard on Adam as it was on us. Uncle Sam doesn't really take into account little brothers when he calls one to serve. Matthew knew how it felt having someone leave the family to join the military because he'd been through it. Not only had *he* been through it, but he had also watched me go through it as well. As we sat in the restaurant, it was the power of that memory that hung in the air.

I had a split second while my head was down on that table to ask the Holy Spirit to once again let me respond with what my baby boy needed and not let my emotions and my feelings be the boss. As I lifted my head to face the music, Matthew began to confirm what my intuition told me was coming. Matthew told us that the call was from the recruiter. Someone had dropped out of the program he was hoping to get into, and a slot had opened up. The recruiter explained to Matthew that these slots fill quickly and that if Matthew wanted it, he needed to head down straight away to sign. Matthew, still looking at me, told us he wasn't going down there unless I went with him. I looked across the table at my husband. I saw his eyes looking straight into my soul. He knows me better than anyone on this earth. I know he was seeing the tornado of thoughts and emotions whipping around inside of me even though I was remaining dead calm on the outside. He didn't say any words, but what I found in his eyes was the strength I needed to calm the storm within. I pulled from him the courage I needed to move from this place I felt frozen in. We both knew I had to go. I looked back at my son, and I saw so much hope! So much excitement! This was it. I knew he was born for this. I also saw the hesitation and reservations all over his face. He was waiting for what I immediately recognized, having been down this road before. He was waiting for his mother's blessing. "Okay. Let's go," was all I needed to say. He immediately called back to tell the recruiter that we were on our way.

Matthew stuffed his lunch down his throat; I mostly moved mine around on my plate. My husband gave an affirmative hug and encouragement to our son as he returned to work. Then Matthew and I climbed into his truck, and away we went. As we started down the road, my son reached over and grabbed my hand. He held it the entire way to that recruiter's office. It was about a thirty-minute drive. We didn't say much to each other. It was mostly silence; He with his thoughts and me with mine. But his grip on my hand never loosened. He, like his brother, knew this was a big ask for his mama. A huge, HUGE ask. Somehow though, that grip on my hand made me stronger than I thought I could be. I was able to sneak a photo of the moment. I knew this was going to be a big day for my son, and the fact he didn't want to do it without me filled my heart to the brim.

On that thirty-minute drive, I was recalling what I had put him through, having had to watch me grieve when Adam left. I knew that was what was playing over in his memory as well. He was afraid to break his mother's heart. I needed him to know I would do better this time around. Like with Adam, I had complete peace about releasing him into God's hands even if I hated where I was releasing him to. Divine peace doesn't come when all the emotions and feelings are on point. Or when trouble, chaos, or tense situations cease. Divine peace comes in most powerfully when those things are at their pinnacle. When everywhere you look, nothing looks like peace. THAT is when divine peace reaches in. I was the last thing I wanted him to worry about. I needed him to know that I was going to be okay; I was stronger this time around. I knew that my hope was Jesus Christ. I had learned how to release my children to God, no matter how difficult it may seem. I had been through the cycle in Romans 5.

...because we know that suffering produces perseverance; perseverance, character; and character, hope. And hope does not disappoint us because God has poured out his love into our hearts by the Holy Spirit, whom he has given us.

ROMANS 5:3-5

I went through the broken heart "suffering" valley when we sent our first son into the Navy. Persevering in the climb out of that valley built in my character a greater truth of who God is, and I grew stronger. Every time you cycle through it, your hope gets bigger. Hope builds upon itself because it cannot disappoint. I could do this. I might not like it, but I knew I'd get through this valley too.

Now faith is being sure of what we hope for
and certain of what we do not see.

HEBREWS 11:1

What is it we hope for? Be sure of *that*! I had been hoping that my son would find direction with the Lord. I had faith he'd find his way. I could not see how the military would fulfill his calling and destiny, but I was certain God was leading him, and since God had never disappointed me yet, that is where my faith and hope would remain.

When we arrived at the recruiter's office, we were greeted at the door and ushered over to the same desk, and sat in the same chairs that we had sat in the day before. The recruiter was on one side of the desk, Matthew and I on the other. The recruiter began to pull out paper after paper, going over this and that, telling Matthew what was next and what it would look like. He went over the timeline for basic training and the extensive training that would follow. It was a lot of information. My head was swirling. I still felt like throwing up. When he was finally finished, he looked at Matthew and asked if he had any questions. Matthew didn't have any.

Then that recruiter looked at me. He told me that he knew it was a lot of information for me to take in and that he understood this was a big assignment to let your child sign on for. He told me he wanted to answer any questions I had. I don't remember having any. I just remember being really appreciative that he would recognize me and affirm how hard this was for me. I thanked him for that. He then scooped up a bunch of Go Army promotional items and handed them to me. A pen, a shirt, a golf towel, and stickers. A peace offering, I guess. He must have thought free stuff would lessen the blow. With that, he slid the papers across the desk and handed my son a pen. Matthew took the pen, pulled the papers toward himself, and set the tip of his pen to the paper. Then my son did something I did not expect. In all of his excitement and readiness to do this, he paused. He laid that pen down on that recruiter's metal desk, turned to face me, took both of my hands in his, and right there in an office full of military personnel said these words, "I am not signing this without your blessing."

Oh wow! I thought my heart was as full as it could get on the ride down, but now I was certain it would burst. My son stood at the place he'd been dreaming about since he was seven years old, and he was willing to walk away from that to save my heart from pain. To have your son love you enough to walk away from his dreams is a love I am not worthy of. A love I do not deserve. I have no words to tell you what I felt, but he gave me a gift I will always treasure. For as long as I live, I will never forget it. It was a really big moment. It was deeper than I think he even understood. I had been gifted this child straight from God's hand. His name means "gift of Yahweh." He had become part of the fabric that made me who I was intended to be since before I had been formed in my mother's womb. Now, without him realizing it, Matthew was calling me up to my God-designed position as a double Blue Star mom. What I heard Matthew saying through his actions was, "Are you ready to let me go?" In my spirit, I heard the Holy Spirit say, "You are ready. Let him go." I am all choked up now as I write about this moment. It was powerful. Moments with the Holy Spirit always are. And this moment, there in the recruiter's office, the Holy Spirit was doing a work, in both of us.

The truth was, I *was* much stronger than I had been the first time around. I will never get used to the idea that my son will be running straight into harm's way, risking his only life to save the lives of others. That is never going to be fun, and a part of me will always hate it. But I did feel strong enough to know that Matthew had to go. If this is the path God had laid out for him, it's where he had to be. And after he was gone, as much as I thought I might not, I knew I was going to survive this.

I looked straight back at Matthew as he waited for my answer. I was so proud of him! I was so happy he had found the strength and faith in his own wings to make this gigantic, terrifying leap from the nest. He knew his wings were strong enough for this flight as long as I let him go, as long as he got my blessing. I wanted this moment to be amazing for him, and I also wanted to share it with him without letting the enemy steal it with pity and fear and whatever else does not come from Heaven. It was a moment of excitement and opportunity and a forward motion into his destiny. It's everything he'd wanted for so long. I could not wait to see how high he was going to fly! I was so, so happy for him. As the bittersweet tears streamed down my face, I gave him the best gift I had to give him. I let him go. With an affirmative nod, an encouraging smile, and with a catch in my throat, I said, "Boy! You've been dreaming of this day since you were seven years old. There is no way I'm stopping you now!" And with that, he gave a big ol' smile, let go of my hands, took the pen, and signed those papers.

I don't think that that recruiter had ever seen anything quite like what he'd just witnessed, and he was taken aback. It made me smile to know my son had just demonstrated a portion of the Father's love in that room.

Matthew was loving me past the point of my broken heart so that we could move forward together yet separate. What I learned the first time through is that with my blessing, I get to go with my sons to all the places I cannot physically go. The anointing of my prayers and the protection of the Father cover them as they go. This was the place Matthew was meant to go. His boots were about to be on many foreign soils, the places he was born to be. I was born to be his military mama, and I would start by claiming the lands and every place he was about to set his feet.

Everything happened very quickly after that. He signed those initial papers on January 22nd, he was sworn in at MEPS in Lansing, Michigan on January 29th, and on February 17th, 2015, I handed my second child- my baby - off to Uncle Sam. My social media post on that day was, "God bless America. You now have both of my babies defending her." When Matthew and God had this journey settled in his heart, God opened doors for him very quickly. I think that was a large part of what got me through, having to settle it in my own heart. The way God was moving him so quickly to the next place. If God wants to get you places, He will get you there. And get him there He did! In less than a month's time!

You'd think that once you've done the letting go once, it would get easier to let go all the subsequent times to come. It isn't. Stronger yes, easier no. My military mom motto has always been, "It doesn't get easier; you just get stronger." Letting go this time, I had to come to terms with the greater level of danger involved. This was dangerous. This was no joke. He was intentionally going to be putting himself in harm's way for the safety of the troops he would be serving with and ultimately for our nation.

...for the Lord Almighty will care for his flock, the house of Judah, and make them like a proud horse in battle.

ZECHARIAH 10:3B

A proud horse in battle. A war horse. A war horse doesn't flinch and doesn't back down when the mortars start flying, or when cannons get launched, or when the smoke that would drive any lesser horse away in fear fills the air. All of those things actually *propel* a war horse forward towards the fight.

The passage in Zechariah talks about the "house of Judah." Jesus is from the house, or tribe, of Judah. You can find His lineage in the gospels of Matthew and Luke. Revelations 5:5 refers to Jesus as the Lion of Judah. So, if Jesus is from the line of Judah, and His blood now flows in our veins as believers and new creations in Christ, this verse applies to us as well. The passage is Zechariah talking about the way He cares and protects Judah's lineage. This includes me. This includes my son. This includes you. This includes your children. Not only will He care for us, but He will make us like war horses.

When God formed the earth, He began by speaking things into existence. At His spoken Word, the earth came to be. "Let there be light"- and there was, and on and on it went for five days. But, on day six, when it came to creating man, God's heart was that we would know Him by more than just His spoken word but also by His love and His touch. So with His two hands, He lovingly formed us and created us in His image. Then He blew his Yahweh breath into our lungs, and we came to be. Every one of us has

God's DNA running through us. It pulses and flows through our veins. You are part of His lineage. The very beat of God's heart beats in yours. Just like the heartbeat of an acorn is to one day become a mighty oak, each of us has a beat inside of us to become something mighty in the Kingdom. When we step into our God-appointed destiny, we begin to represent Him and His heart wherever He places our feet. If you're a doctor, you are a doctor with a heart that beats the same as His, and you represent Him there with your patients and their families. If you are a teacher, you teach from the beat of His heart in your chest, and you represent Him to your students, other faculty, school board, and community. When we walk in the ordained steps and destiny He has for us, wherever that may be, He will not only care for us as His flock, but He releases an anointing over us for us to become war horses in that place. We are equipped for whatever battle lies ahead of us in that place because we were *created* for it—created to be His ambassadors, His regents, His image for that very place. If God has called your son or daughter to be part of the United States Military, then you need to understand He has created them to be there. They are equipped to be there. They are supposed to be there. And if they are in the military, then that means *you* are created and equipped to be a military mom.

There was something beating in Matthew's heart before he ever took a breath on this earth. Something God put in him, a beat and rhythm that matched that of God's heart. It was a beat that would get his boots on many foreign soils. Matthew has the heartbeat of a war horse. When he signed those papers, it was not so much a signed contract with the United States of America as it was fulfilling his calling as a representative of the Kingdom of God. It was his Kingdom contract. He was created to represent the

Kingdom inside the United States Army. He has been given footing in a place that I will never get with people I will never see. With both of my sons, I have watched how God has strategically placed them exactly where they've needed to be for that particular moment. Whether it is for safety, or favor, or blessing, God aligns their steps. He opens doors, and He closes them. As long as they continue to let God lead them, they will be cared for and made into proud horses in battle. Unflinching, unwavering, run towards the battle, war horses. God has already lined up the victories for my sons. I just have to let them run to the battle.

God showed me that my sons would always be safer in His will, in His placement, than they could ever be in mine. While my placement may look safer according to the world's standards or by my mama standards, it is far more dangerous for him to be out of alignment with the Lord. The most important thing to me was that I raise my boys to know and accept Jesus Christ as their personal Lord and Savior. Now that they have that, I have to trust God to take them from there. Trust God when He says that He will care for His flock, your children. Not only care for them, but He will make them warriors for the Kingdom. Unflinching, unwavering, run towards the battle, come out as victors, war horses. Whatever heartbeat they have, whatever God has put inside of them, He put it there to match the beat of His own heart. The heartbeat to become something mighty for the Kingdom. God will not set them up to fail. In His calling is their safest place.

THOUGHTS

THOUGHTS

five

ROCKS & LILIES

WAY BACK WHEN MY CHILDREN were still very young, I went on a walk with the Lord. It was a long, winding, rough terrain journey through the land of worry, and it was not fun. I won't go into all the details as I am sure everyone reading this has been through a stage where worry has wanted to build a house in your life and has consumed your thoughts, your rest, your actions, your peace, and the very way you move through life from day to day. It is vicious and unrelenting. Everything came pushing in on me at the same time, and I was completely overwhelmed. I had been walking through this land for months. It finally got so bad that one day I found myself literally hiding from the world under my husband's blueprint table, sobbing out to God. I was crippled by the weight of worry, and I knew that God was the only one who could get me out of there. It was during this crippled moment while my desperate cries were being sent up to the Lord in gulps and sobs that He brought a scripture to mind.

. . . the punishment that brought us peace was upon him. . .

ISAIAH 53:5B

And just like that, I had this Holy moment of clarity. That was it! I got it! There are times that it has taken me a span of time to grab ahold of something from Heaven, and then there are times like this when a Kingdom truth downloads into my spirit from His Spirit, and I get it instantly. Everything I could not see because of the thick cloud of worry surrounding me suddenly came slamming into focus as that cloud was replaced with a wind of truth that blew the lies of the enemy clear out of sight. The language of God is not restricted to human words. When He reveals a truth, it can often be told to us without Him uttering one human word. He didn't tell me a parable or layout a five-step program. All I know is I went from a sobbing, blubbering mess in one moment to a jumping, rejoicing, praising out of my mind with excitement victor in the next. It changed my life forever.

Worry is an attack of the enemy. It's a good one too, *if* we let it be effective in our lives, and I had. I had allowed worry and had given it permission to keep me on this hideous, dark, disgusting path, barely moving and at times even crippling me to a standstill. Worry had robbed hope from me. Worry had robbed faith from me. Worry had robbed Jesus from me. I had let worry be the leader in my life, allowing it to surround me and drag me down a dark road. Though I still had sight of the hem of His garment, the worry was leading me away from Him.

God had shown me that I was actually hanging on tighter to the hand of worry instead of holding on to the hand of the Father who loves me enough to send His son to die in my place. Holding onto worry's hand was separating me from Him. I was essentially believing the lie that His love for me and the work of the Cross was not big enough to cover all the troubling bits and pieces in my life. With my actions, if not with my words, I was saying that worry would do more for me than He ever could.

When that wave of understanding washed over me, I went into warrior mode. Not only did I repent for wrong believing, I immediately grabbed ahold of His promise of peace. That word peace is actually *shalom*. It is used 237 times in the Old Testament, and it is packed with meaning. Safe, well, happy, friendly, welfare, health, prosperity, peace, completeness, soundness, and favor. Come on! That is what was bought on the Cross for us! If a portion of the work of the Cross was for me to have *shalom* peace and then, in turn, *be* a place and person of peace, then I was going to have to go after it. Whatever He has for me, I want it. And I wanted peace.

When I started my fight for peace, I found myself in the book of Matthew. Matthew 6:25-34 contains the red letters, which are the words of Jesus Christ telling us, "do not worry." He talks about my value being higher than everything else God created. If He feeds and cares for the birds, how much more will He care for me? Then He talks about the lilies and what they are *not* doing. They are not toiling (laboring) or spinning.

See how the lilies of the field grow. They do not labor or spin. Yet I tell you that not even Solomon in all this splendor was dressed like one of these. If that is how God clothes the grass of the field, which is here today and tomorrow thrown into the fire, will he not much more clothe you, O you of little faith?

MATTHEW 6:28-30

Lilies! Jesus points to the lilies as the place that I should set my gaze, and then I should learn from their example. This launched me into a search to find out why. Here are some interesting facts I discovered. Wild lilies are perennial plants and will grow without intervention or help from humans. They are incredible pollinators and attract insects with their large beautiful flowers. When I looked into "thrown into the fire," I found that the lilies that would grow in the fields Jesus is referencing would be gathered up with grasses and used as tinder for fires in the winter season. Amazing! These precious lilies that are more splendid by God's design than Solomon could ever be dressed in his finest garb are just doing what God designed them to do. They are growing in a field in all their splendor and do not have a care in the world. They are not thinking about what the weeds are doing growing beside them. They are not looking to the skies for rain or wondering when the sun will shine again. They aren't concerned with the soil composition in which they have taken root. They are just being lilies! I wanted this carefree, peaceful, worry-free life of a lily, and these two verses were telling me I could have it!

I was determined to be a lily and just do what I was designed to do. I wanted to be who God designed me to be without my human interference getting in the way. My human worry will never do anything to aid my circumstances. Only by letting Him be my source and my *everything* would I thrive. I wanted to attract others to the beauty of my Savior and His goodness in my life, just like the petals of this flower. I wanted my life to show that what I have with Christ as my Savior is far greater than what I do or do not possess on this earth. And if, through my obedience of just learning from the lilies of the field, I could produce a tinder to ignite the hearts of others for the glory of God, then this was worth grabbing onto. I was going to learn to grow where He had planted me and let Him hold my days in His hands. I was going to let Him be my sun and my rain and my soil composition. If lilies don't worry, I wasn't going to either. I was going to set my face on Him and let Him do the rest.

———————————

But seek first his kingdom and his righteousness, and all these things will be given to you as well. Therefore do not worry about tomorrow, for tomorrow will worry about itself.

MATTHEW 6:33-34

———————————

I wanted this to be a pillar of truth established in my life. I *needed* it to be. I never wanted to be found hiding in a heap under the table again, so debilitated from the lies of hell that I could not face the day. I had to be intentional. I had to learn to be a lily. I was up for the fight. I was going to war with all I had to kick worry back to the gates of hell where it had come from.

When your default setting has been to allow worry to creep in and then to grab ahold of it like a friend once it gets in there, it takes practice to reset your default setting. I knew this is what was meant in Romans 12:2, which tells you and me to *"be transformed by the renewing of your mind."* I had come to understand that anything that separates me from God is a sin in my life. When we choose to worry, it separates us from Him. To worry is a choice, even though it may feel like it just creeps in. Jesus also makes this pretty clear when in those red letters, He clearly says, "do not." If He says "do not," and I do it, I am choosing to sin. Remaining in the land of worry was a sin. It was separating me from God, and if He is not in the place I am, I don't ever want to be there.

"

Remaining in the
land of worry
was a sin. It was
separating me from
God, and if the is
not in the place I am,
I don't ever want to
be there.

———————

Sometimes I find that the easiest way to make something that is spiritual impact me in the natural is to do something tangible. I needed to do something in the physical that would represent what was going on in the spiritual. This is a way to pull down "on earth as it is in Heaven." So, I went outside, and I got a rock. A good size rock. One that took my whole hand to hold it. It had some weight. Then I painted it red to represent the blood of Jesus, and I placed it on my desk where I would see it every day, pretty much all day long. It became my greatest weapon to get the Cross-bought peace cemented into my life. Every time something would come up that had the potential to throw me into the old default of worry, I would pick up that red rock and assign that name, that event, that happening or moment to that rock. Some of the names I gave that rock were money, business, my boys, other family members or issues, new tires, weather, health, or whatever came up that had the potential to bring on even a hint of worry. That name went on that rock. I'd pick up that rock, speak the name of whatever over it, and hold it in my hand. Then I imagined myself throwing that rock at Jesus while He was hanging on the Cross and telling Him that what He was doing on the Cross wasn't big enough to cover whatever it was that was trying to present itself in my life as worry. This was incredibly powerful, and let me tell you, it didn't take long for me to get the new default of peace in my life. My goodness, every time I would even try to imagine myself doing that to Him, I would become broken before Him at the price He had paid for me. I would never, COULD never do that in person. I would never throw a rock at Jesus and say, "what you're doing isn't big enough to cover my checkbook, or my family, or my illness." But that is EXACTLY what I was doing in the spirit every time I chose to worry. I know that what He bought for me and the victories He won on my behalf are more than enough to cover anything I may face in this world.

His final words on the Cross were, "it is finished." This means the price He paid covers it all. His blood-bought peace is my spiritual promise of God. So, if there were no way I would say those insulting words of unbelief and throw rocks at Him in the natural, there was going to be no way I was going to continue to do this in the spiritual. Instead, I focused on His promises and on seeking first His Kingdom while countering everything the enemy or the world threw at me by covering it with His Word.

For example, if I had labeled the rock with an illness, I countered it with *"by His wounds, I am healed"* (Isaiah 53:5). If it was finances, I countered with *"my God will meet all your needs according to the riches of His glory"* (Philippians 4:19).

The enemy is a liar, and when confronted with the truth of the Word, he has to flee and take his lie of worry with him. The "blood" I had painted on the rock reminded me He had already won this battle against the enemy.

I was given a new understanding of how much God loves me, and I was completely undone by it. He loves me so very much that while I was still a sinner and I did not even know His name, He took my worry to the Cross and destroyed it so I would never have to carry it again. I didn't deserve that. I still don't, and I never will. None of us do. But that is the power of His love for us.

In a short amount of time, instead of going through the motions of having to physically pick up that rock and hold it in my hand, all I would have to do is glance at it, and I would hear Him speak to my spirit,

" *Don't worry. I love you. Remember the lilies.*

I would remember the lilies, and I would remember His love for me was so much greater than His love for them that these God thoughts would drive the worry from my life. Worry was not just gone; it was completely obliterated from my life. His love and peace cover me. He is forever faithful, and He has not once, not ever, failed me yet!

Fast forward to several years later, and you'll find me as a mom with *both* sons in the military and stretched to what I think is my limit. My strength was wavering and waning day by day. My oldest son was stationed in Japan and often deployed out on an aircraft carrier somewhere in the great China Sea. My youngest son was in basic training. I was waiting in what seemed like suspended time for the boot camp letters from my youngest son to start arriving. There had been no news or contact from him since he had left home. The mail system at the base where he was training was having difficulties, and his letters were far later getting home to us than his brother's letters had been. My oldest son's ship often went without internet for safety reasons, and of course, there is no cell service out in the middle of the ocean. I had had no news; No news from the sea, and no news from land. I was hanging on by my last tattered thread. There is a fine line between wonder and worry, and my wonder was slipping into worry.

When the mail did finally arrive, it was a letter from basic training. Just seeing the letter in the mailbox alone gave me the strength to catch a breath, a breath that I felt like I had been holding this entire time. As I sat down and started reading through the letter, anxious to see how my baby boy was doing, I was undone again by the Father's love for me and for my boys.

There at the bottom of Matthew's letter home, written on digi-camo Army stationary, he had penned these words:

God had given me an incredible gift years before by getting me through the lie of worry by teaching me how to view it through the work of the Cross and from the lilies. He knew then that I would need this victory years down the road when both of my sons were serving in the US military. He knew I would have to be able to hand up my sons to Him and let Him carry them instead of succumbing to my worry. He is such an incredibly good Father who made sure I had this promise woven into the threads of who I am before I ever got to this point in my life when both of my sons would be in the military. When I was stretched with the toughest act of surrender to date and hanging on by one tattered thread, all He had to do was remind me of this victory and how we had already won it for my life and the lives of my sons years before. He did it with five words written by the hand of my son.

These were not Matthew's words. They were God-breathed words given to Matthew just for me. Matthew had no idea of the journey to defeat worry that I had previously been traveling. He was much too young when it happened. He also had no idea how these words would impact me when I read them. Only God could have given me this wink from Heaven through my son's letter. He is forever with us. We just have to look for Him.

When I prayed and asked God what the title of this book would be if ever He fulfilled the process of getting it all the way to print, the period in my life when I battled to defeat worry and learned about the lilies came to mind. I spent some time digging once again into these lilies Jesus spoke of. What I found this time is that the Hebrew definition for the flower or the lily Jesus was probably referring to is called a "red anemone." When I looked up the red anemone to see what it looked like, it then became crystal clear what the title of this book would be. These lilies in the field Jesus is referring to are red, white, and blue! If ever there was a flower meant for military moms, I dare say this would be it. I also found that these lilies do not like to grow solo, but if planted in groups, they will flourish! Ladies, He has the same message for you:

Don't worry. I love you. Remember the lilies.

What was accomplished on the Cross covers you, and it covers our children wherever they are. We cannot be effective in our anointing when we are paralyzed with worry. It separates us from God and keeps us from walking in His promise of peace. Let's get rid of that one, ladies! We don't have time for that lie. We need to learn from the lilies and remember that He will take care of us. All we have to do is grow where He has planted us. As military moms, we are growing here together, and in this place, we will flourish! Not only that, our obedience can, in turn, become the tinder for others' hearts to catch the flame of the King and the peace He bought for them. Our children included.

After we read about the peace Jesus bought on the Cross in Isaiah 53, if we keep reading, we find there is a bit more to this promise that opens up in Isaiah 54.

> *Though the mountains be shaken and the hills be removed, yet my unfailing love for you will not be shaken, nor my covenant of peace be removed," says the Lord, who has compassion on you. "O afflicted one, lashed by storms and not comforted, I will <u>build</u> you with stones of turquoise, your foundations with sapphires. I will make your battlements of rubies, your gates of sparkling jewels, and all your walls of precious stones. All your sons will be taught by the Lord, great will be your children's peace."*
>
> ISAIAH 54:10-13

Everything around us might feel like a storm that is lashing and shaking us about. It's in those times when He is pointing us back to His unending covenant of peace. *"I will build you."* I underlined the word *build* because it is important that we understand what God is doing in these verses. That word actually means to lie down, made to rest. That same Hebrew word, *rabats,* is found in Psalm 23:2, *"He makes me <u>lie down</u> in green pastures."* What God is actually doing is building us to be a people that can lie down in His peace when everything around us is being shaken. The beauty of who we are meant to be- structures of sapphires, jewels, and stones painted by His own hand - is who we will become when we walk in this covenant. This is the beauty that will attract others as we are beacons of peace with sunrises of rubies in the midst of storms. ***"All your sons will be taught by the Lord, great will be your children's peace."*** I just want to add several exclamation points right there! My sons, your sons, your daughters will be taught by the Lord, and they too will walk in this same peace! And all we have to do to have this covenant promise fulfilled in our lives and in theirs is to stop worrying and lie down in peace. Let Him carry the weight, the worry, the unknown. It seems such a simple thing to do, yet it can be so hard to attain. Hebrews 4:11 tells us we must "labor to enter into that rest." We have to fight for it. For ourselves, for others looking for a beacon in their storm, and for our children.

One of the enemy's greatest tricks is to entice us into the worry ring with him. Once we are in there, he can deliver blow after blow as we dance around with him in his ring. His goal, as with any boxer, is to knock us out. All we can do is try to keep our face covered, stay upright, and remain in the fight. While in this ring, he makes it his ultimate goal that all of our focus remains on him and on trying to dodge and recover from his next move. If he succeeds, he knows we will not be looking at Jesus. The way we win is to never get in this ring to start with. The moment we have the thoughts of worry about our military children or any other matter, we should train ourselves to hear the starting bell from hell alerting us that the round is starting with the enemy's gloved hands waiting to pummel us, and then our response needs to be, "Not today satan. My child is a child of the most high King, and this fight was already won at the Cross. I choose peace. IT IS FINISHED!"

As our sons or daughters are called to various military posts, we are going to be called to various posts as well. Right now, our post is military mom. Fierce, mama bear, the devil doesn't get to mess with my kids, military mom. We need to be advancing and taking ground. We cannot allow the devil to distract us. His weapon of worry is only powerful if we let it be. So let's not let it. Don't get in his ring. God will carry everything we need to get us through today, and He will carry it all again to get us through tomorrow. His love for us is that great.

The punishment that brought us peace was upon Him.

ISAIAH 53:5B

Let Him be your sun and your rain and your soil composition. Set your face on Him, and let Him do the rest. Remember the lilies.

THOUGHTS

THOUGHTS

six

GRIT & GRACE

ONE OF MY FAVORITE Chinese proverbs is, "out of the hottest fire comes the strongest steel." I find it fascinating for some reason that metal, when forged with fire, comes out stronger. It changes the microstructure of the metal to improve strength, hardness, toughness, ductility, and corrosion resistance. When sorting through the pictures in my mind to find one that would represent this proverb, I always pull forward the sword. A mighty sword. One like Goliath's, maybe. The one David sees and says to the priest in 1 Samuel 21:9, "there is none like it." I picture my sword, the one I carry as a Spirit-filled Shield-maiden as described at the beginning of this book. It's powerful, strong, sharp, and heavy. Only those who are willing to fight for His Kingdom will ever learn to wield it well. I am so willing! More than anything, I want to learn how to take the land for the King. To fight the darkness, free His people and bring to them the light and love of who He is. It takes time in His presence, counsel, and teaching for me to learn to hold it, wield it, and be effective for the Kingdom of God. There are days that I slay the enemy from the moment my boots hit the boards, and then there are days I feel clumsy and awkward and not strong enough to even lift it. There is still so much for me to learn.

When I couple that Chinese proverb with 1 Corinthians 3:10-15, I realize there is something else to be learned about the power of fire. This passage indicates that only the things of God remain after the testing by fire. I think these two ideas go hand in hand. When I look at the times I have been through the fire with God I realize that I do come out stronger, and only the things of Him remain. Everything that is left behind, burnt up, or removed is exposed for what it is - dross. I cannot have a strong sword for battle if the dross remains.

In metalworking, the raw form of metal is placed into a crucible. As that crucible is heated at incredibly hot temperatures, the impurities, the dross, rises to the top. As it rises, the metalsmith will skim or pour these impurities off of the top of the molten metal. Google dictionary lists the definition of dross as something regarded as worthless or rubbish.

Remove the dross from the sliver, and a silversmith

can produce a vessel...

PROVERBS 25:4

We are going to go through some tough circumstances, some rough moments, some hot fires on this military journey, and our children are as well. The way we are going to get through these tough times is to believe that once we come out the other side, God will have made us stronger than when we went in. In that fire, we will be refined. If we are going to be shield-maidens and powerful warriors, who wield swords of the strongest caliber, we have to let Him remove the dross that would hinder our God missions.

Crucible, according to the Merriam-Webster Dictionary, is a place or situation in which concentrated forces interact to bring about change. The military, I found, is definitely a crucible of fire. You will not come out of this the same way you went in, and neither will your children. This is going to test you on all levels- mentally, physically, emotionally, and spiritually. It will require more fortitude and strength than you've probably ever utilized. But keep in mind, your children are going through it as well. Ready yourselves for battle because there is nothing you can do to stop it. You have to go *through* it in order to come *out* of it.

When Adam arrived at Great Lakes Naval Station just north of Chicago for RTC (Recruit Training Command), better known as basic training, he was allowed to make one two-minute phone call home. He was only permitted to tell us four pieces of information: he arrived safely, the next phone call would be in approximately three weeks, he would be sending home a box with his personal belongings, and a letter would arrive shortly containing his mailing address and graduation information. I was able to quickly add at the end of this phone call, "I love you, you got this, shine bright, we are praying you through," and then he was gone.

Within a few days of him leaving, that box he had spoken of arrived. Every article of his clothing, his overnight bag, cell phone, and anything that said "Adam" was in that box. I hated that box. I pulled out the articles one at a time and imagined what it might have been like for him to box everything up and seal it in that box. He was completely stripped of everything and anything that may have had a stamp of normal or security. Maybe I was overthinking it. I don't know. Going through the items, I noticed one of his pant legs had been rolled up just one time, but it was one big roll to well above the knee. I later found out many of the recruits' pants came home that way. During their intake process, each recruit is required to roll up a pant leg and then stand on a machine that scans and measures their feet for the best fitting shoe. It is such a rushed, hurried, chaotic yell fest that they don't have time to roll the pant leg back down before taking the pants off and placing them in that box. From there, it is just a rush of madness getting the recruits all set up for the next eight weeks. They are kept up that entire first night and all the next day for in-processing. It has only just begun.

Of course, I didn't know any of this at the time it was going on; all I had was a box. My thoughts ran wild, and I was trying to brace myself for what may come home in the boot camp letters. I had no idea what to expect. Or maybe I did, but I was trying to convince myself it was going to be rainbows and lollipops. Well, it wasn't. When his letters started coming home, he pretty much hated his life. No surprise. His first letter started with "The first three days were the worst days of my life," and he went on to tell us just how awful it was for him. He said he wasn't surprised by it either, but still, he was not enjoying his first few days with Uncle Sam.

The first response you have when you hear your child is hurting or in a bad headspace, no matter their age or place in life, is the mama bear rising up in you, and you want to fix it. It's who we are as nurturers, caregivers, protectors. I have a running joke with my now-adult children when something isn't going their way. When they are all done venting and telling me about the atrocities that they are going through, I ask them, "Who can I call?" Now, they, as well as I realize there is no one I can call, but sometimes I think it's nice for them to know I *would* call someone and I *would* fix it if I could. The thought is still there, no matter how silly the notion may be. Reading these letters from boot camp, no matter how awful his experience was going to be, I knew this was *his* journey. There was nobody I could call. He had to walk it. He had five weeks left from the date of that first letter.

Sometimes we have to go *through* it in order to come *out* of it. There are times that God will prevent something difficult or threatening from coming our way and stop it dead in its tracks. Sometimes we realize exactly when that's happening, and we can see the goodness of our Father. So we praise Him for sparing us. I also believe there are many times He has spared us from things and situations that we will never know about on this side of Heaven. One day we will be blown away when we see all He has done. Then there are times He allows us to go through it. There is a strength that only comes when we go through that fire. The strength we get from *that* fire He knows we will need down the road on the other side. He is preparing us, strengthening us for what lies ahead in our journey that is unbeknownst to us. Just like metal forged in fire, we are forged as well. Whatever Adam needed for what lay ahead for him, he wasn't going to get it unless he went through this fire.

Daniel 3:8-30 tells the story of Shadrach, Meshach, and Abednego. These three Hebrew boys refused to bow down and worship a false god as decreed by the wicked king. The punishment for disobeying the king was to be burnt in the furnace. Now God is pretty big. He could have done anything that would have prevented them from facing this fate. God could have somehow stopped them from having to go into the fire, but He didn't. Instead of preventing it, He had them go through it so that when they came out, the truth that He is a God who saves was greater and stronger than it had been before they went in. There was strength on the other side. Not only did God spare their lives and protect them so that not a hair on their heads was singed in that furnace (a furnace so hot the soldiers throwing them into the flames died on the spot), but the wicked king said from his own lips, "no other god can save this way." What an awesome revelation! Come on! A declaration of the saving power of the one true God coming from this wicked king's lips! All because God allowed these boys to go through it. Had God prevented them from going through it, the king may never have been saved. Now let's not skip a very important part of the story. After these boys were thrown in the furnace to be burnt alive, an incredible discovery was made in the process. When the wicked king looked into that fire to witness what he believed would be their imminent death, he and his advisors didn't just see three boys; they saw four people! God was in those fires with them! If God allows you to go through it, I promise you, He is going in with you.

Whatever God was doing with Adam, I'll admit I still didn't completely understand it all, but I knew he had to go through it. I also knew that God was right there going through it with him. And while Adam was in this crucible with the Lord, I was praying and believing that He would skim the dross off of Adam's life and bring out the purest form of who He created Adam to be. Adam was being forged in fire, and so was I.

Brace yourselves because you are about to realize a new meaning of two words: grit and grace. I am not sure what has or will come home to you in the form of a boot camp letter, but you may be surprised. What I found from both of my boys in their letters home was complete, vulnerable freedom to express some of their deepest emotions and feelings. Right now, while in basic training, they are all in with mental and physical fortitude. They are digging deep and bringing every last ounce of sheer will and want-to into this experience. It's tough. They are running on pure grit.

They are not allowed to talk. To anyone. Ever. They are not allowed to have feelings or thoughts of their own. They are told what to do all the time. Every day. They are told what to wear, even down to the undergarments. They are told what to eat, when to eat, how to eat, and how fast to eat. They are told when to sleep and when to get up, which usually comes from being startled awake at all hours of the night with obnoxious shouting and noise. They are wrong about everything all the time, and there is no reprieve. They are exhausted, yelled at, beaten down physically and mentally, and they are just trying to get through it. The only place they find anything that resembles peace is when the lights first go out, and they are tucked beneath their scratchy wool blanket. That moment of reprieve from the suck that has been their day is short-lived and would only last a few moments because as they drift off into sleep, their rest remains fitful, knowing at any moment they could be ripped from their beds and drug off into the night to do it all again.

Letters to home were their only place that was safe enough for them to vent and release and do something they weren't allowed to do during basic training—feel and express. We have to cultivate a place of peace and create a safe space for them to do those things. We do that by not responding as the "who can I call" mom. As much as we want to let her, that woman cannot be allowed to speak. She is not helpful, and she will not bring them peace. We have to trust God to be their defender now that we have released our children back to him.

What you may also find in their letters home, as I did, was how God was covering and surrounding them with His grace. His grace is sufficient.

But he said to me, "My grace is sufficient for you, for my power is made perfect in weakness."

2 CORINTHIANS 12:9

When they find themselves in a weak place, that is when the power of His grace kicks in. When they run out of grit, and there is nothing left of themselves to get through it, His grace moves in, and now they are running on grace.

You need to find your grit and grace too. Let God take you into the fires of His crucible, where He can skim the dross out of your life and reveal the purest form of you. This is the best way to be prepared, to wield your sword at whatever is about to come hurling at you.

In the Bible, silver is used a lot as an example of what happens in the refiner's fire. When a silversmith has finished skimming the dross from the silver, he stands back and lets the metal continue to heat in the crucible until it is the correct temperature. The silversmith knows that the silver is ready to fashion into something beautiful when he can see his own reflection in the metal as he looks down into the crucible. This is my heart's cry. I want to sit in the crucible of the Father's love until He sees His reflection on me. Until all the dross is skimmed off and out of my life, and then He is able to look in and say, "Sherry! There you are! I see myself all over you. You are strong. You are who I've called you to be. You are ready. Now, here's your sword. Go and represent me well. Go shine bright. Go be my image everywhere you place your feet."

It would be really easy for me to be the "who can I call parent" and to somehow have the ability to make all the problems go away. But that's not God's way, and when it's not God's way, it can't be my way either. Being that parent is a terrible way to raise children because it puts their faith in some *one* other than God! It would have put my children's faith in me. What an awful outcome that would be! I would have failed them in the worst way. I am not supposed to fill that position in their lives. God is. Going through valleys and hardships and fires are some of the most amazing times when you are able to find that God is so very close to you and that He has never left your side. So, rather than being the "who can I call" parent, what I really need to be is a parent who points the gaze of my children back to Jesus. To bring His peace into the fold. To point out His Grace. To lift their heads, not fuel their frustration. Not rant and rave and carry on. Not feel sorry for them or partner in their pity. All of those things are the dross I leave with the Lord, so what comes out through me during their vulnerable times, what they see in their mom, is Him reflecting through me.

I am not always going to have all the answers, and I may not always know how to respond, but that is when His grace will be sufficient for me. I, too, am running on grit and grace. The more I move with the intent on this, the easier it becomes. Now, you might fall apart behind the scenes, trust me. This I have done many a time. I am only human. You too are only human. But when your kids need you to be strong, you will be because you've gone through it.

When my younger son Matthew went into basic training with the Army, unlike my Navy son, all his personal effects, including his cell phone were stored away until graduation. Nothing got sent home. The cell phones were held under lock and key until the recruits had earned a phone call.

They did not have public payphones as the Navy had. Their cell phones were their only line home. With both of my sons, I was put in contact with other moms who had kids in the same division and company as my boys. When something started happening within those groups, those moms would sound an alarm, and it would go down the chain to other moms.

When Matthew's company had finally earned its first ten-minute call home, the mom alarm was sounded. "Get to your phones. They are calling home!" Oh, my heart! The anticipation and waiting were absolutely brutal. My husband and I waited and waited. Minutes seemed like hours. Other moms were reporting back that they had talked to their sons or daughters and how great it was to hear their voices. I was still pacing my living room. I knew time was running out. Where was he? With only two minutes left on the clock, my phone rang. It was not his cell number, but there was no way I was not going to answer! When I said "hello," all I heard on the other end were gulps and tears. It was him. Ladies, I am here to tell you, this was a moment it took everything I had to steel myself, to find the grit, and to walk completely in His grace. I did not know what was happening on the other end of that phone, but I was determined to be my son's peace and safe place. I was not going to fall apart now. I was going to be strong for him, and the only way I would accomplish that was by asking the Holy Spirit to bring through me what my son needed most for those two minutes. Matthew told me in broken sentences that his cell phone wasn't working, and he had to wait for someone to finish a call home before he could ask to borrow a phone and call us. He followed that by telling me he was okay, and that was about all he could get out. And with a strength that I did not own or carry myself,

I just started talking. The words just started coming out. Encouraging, happy, Holy Spirit words were just rolling off my tongue. I told him how proud we were of him. I told him to keep going that this too shall pass. I told him that he was in it to win it and that he had this all the way to the end. I told him we were praying for him every day and that God did not bring him this far to let him fall now. He was a Motcheck, and he was walking in the steps ordered by God. I gave him the countdown of days and reminded him that he was one day closer to done. I told him we loved him and that he was never, not for one minute, in this alone. And then, through his tears, he said, "I love you, too," and that was the end of the call.

As I hung up the phone, I turned and looked at my husband, Mike. The man that has always steadied me and empowered me. He is my safe place, my grounding, my constant, my best thing on this side of Heaven. As he read the room, he knew by how I was talking to Matthew on the phone that this was a hard phone call for both of us. He didn't know exactly what had happened on the other end, but he saw in my eyes that I was about to fall to pieces. Mike has always been keenly aware that my emotional state often pivots on his response to any given circumstance that could cause me to blow. There has been a lifetime of moments in which I would look directly at his response to help steady and gauge my own. Mike is rarely rattled or moving at a pace of urgency. When he is or does, we all take notice. He has a way of calming me and stilling my spirit, and even at times simply getting me to remember to breathe. I am so thankful for this man God knew I needed in my life. As I sat on the floor in front of the recliner he was sitting in, he leaned forward, put his hands on my shoulders, and immediately spoke the words, "He's okay. He's going to be okay." I knew he was right, but the tears came anyway. Hearing Matthew's tears on the other end of the phone broke my mama heart to bits. If only my arms could have reached him. OH! That stupid cell phone! I could imagine him sitting and waiting, not even knowing if he would be able to borrow a phone or make a call home. Would anyone have minutes to spare at the end of their call? That, stacked on top of everything he was going through, just broke my heart for him.

I knew I needed to pull myself together and get some perspective, and there was one person I could talk to who could relate to what Matthew was going through. His brother, who was stationed in Japan. When I contacted Adam, he said, "Mom, you have to understand he hasn't been able to talk to anyone this whole time. You aren't allowed to talk, and when you finally hear a voice that's not yelling at you and actually cares, the voice of your mom, it's pretty emotional." Matthew himself said just about those exact words to me a few days later in his letter home.

Don't think because of the phone call I'm having a bad time. I just love my momma.

I have never been in a place when I have felt what Matthew felt while going through basic training. I have never been through something where you get broken down on purpose just to build you back up. I could not relate to or understand this. But God did. He knew exactly what my son was going through because He was walking through this fire with him. He knew what Matthew needed, and the Holy Spirit led me to be a place of peace and encouragement for my son. I was able to point his gaze back to

God and remind him that he is not alone. I was able to quiet "who can I call mom" and let the Holy Spirit do the talking. *That's* what comes out of His fire.

Coming out of the crucible with His reflection is not only the heart cry for myself, but it's also the heart cry for my children. I pray that they would come out of God's refiner's fire, wherever, whenever, and whatever that fire might be, and they would be reflecting the image of Him so brightly that it cannot be hidden. God had called both of my sons to this fire and placed both sets of their feet in the United States Military to be reflections of Him. They were going to come out stronger than when they went in for purposes we did not yet know. And so was I.

As much as we may want to, sometimes we aren't supposed to stop the fire. We are led to go through it, swords in hand for the ground we will gain tomorrow. What I have learned is that typically the fires we are going through today have nothing to do with who we are but are for who we are to become. Today's fires are for victories we will see tomorrow. A wicked king didn't recognize the one true God until after somebody else went through the fire. If the Lord has ordered your children's steps (which He has) and those steps have taken them to the United States Military, no matter what this moment may look like, trust me, they are going to come out of this stronger, closer to God and reflecting His image more than they ever have before going in, and so will you. Not only that, whatever and whoever the fire you just walked through is meant to impact, God will bring it to pass.

You are not in this fire alone, and I want you to know that He will bring you through it. We may not be able to control the circumstances that we find ourselves in, but we can control our reactions to them. When we let Him lead us, we will always find He is far better at navigation than we are. Being a military mom is going to take some grit, but, His grace always has been and forever will be sufficient. He will change the microstructure of who you are to improve your strength, hardness, toughness, ductility, and corrosion resistance. You will be forged in the Holy fires of His love and will come out a stronger, bolder warrior that no enemy wants to reckon with. You will wield the sword with power, with grit, and with grace.

THOUGHTS

THOUGHTS

COBRAS & ANGELS

BACK IN 2012, I HAD THE GREAT PRIVILEGE of going to see Thunder Over Louisville with some of my family, including my daddy, a Viet Nam veteran. Thunder Over Louisville is an amazing celebration that happens during the start of the Kentucky Derby Festival. It hosts the nation's largest annual fireworks event and one of the top five out-of-this-world air shows in the country. I know that's a tall order to fulfill, but it did just that. The air show was six hours long and was followed by the most incredible display of fireworks I have ever seen. The air show included all the past and present aircraft of our military. It had everything from the fixed-wing biplanes of the World Wars to the newest and greatest military aircraft of the twenty-first century, including the Harrier Jump Jet, which does things that will blow your mind. The throngs of people were cheering and clapping throughout the day. The atmosphere was just pulsing with excitement and patriotism as we watched the finest of our country's pilots and aircraft do what they were made to do. The pinnacle of the air show happened just before the twenty-eight-minute fireworks display started. Helicopters flew through the night skies flying the largest American Flag I'd ever seen lit up beneath them. Wow! It was really a day to remember.

As I think back to that day, there is one touchstone moment that will always stand out more than the rest. Amid the noise of jets so loud you could feel them in your chest but moving so fast incredibly fast you found yourself spinning around in circles trying to catch a glimpse, and the eerily silent approach of the stealth bomber as it crept overhead, something happened. Off in the distance we heard a sound. It was faint, but there was no mistaking what it was. A helicopter. The instant that sound of chopper blades drifted to our ears, my daddy stood up. I watched him as he turned and faced the direction that sound was coming from. He stood real straight and tall, and something came across his face. There was no denying he recognized that sound. This skinny chopper made its way towards us, and painted all across the nose of it was the distinguishing, identifying trademark - the shark teeth. When his eyes finally locked onto it as it came into view, he said, "Cobra Gunship!" in a voice of victory. My daddy is a quiet man, and though he didn't do it outwardly, what I saw happening inside him was his fist pumping high in the air and "oh heck yeah!" being shouted from the top of his lungs. There was no doubt that this Cobra was a big deal and meant so much to him.

In 1968, the year my daddy graduated high school, he received a notice in the mail that required him to register at the local post office to be on standby with the United States Selective Service. All American males of draft age received these notices, unlike today's requirement by law that every male file within thirty days of his eighteenth birthday. A few months after he registered with Mrs. Rowe on the second floor of the post office, he was loaded onto a bus full of other men, boys really, and taken to Detroit to have a military physical. Then during the summer of 1969, his name was drawn for the draft. He was going to Viet Nam. After boot camp and specialized training to become an infantry small arms expert, in April of 1970, he was put on a plane and sent to war. He left behind my mother and my older sister, who at the time was only eight weeks old. He would not see his family again until March 14, 1971. A young man of twenty years would spend the next eleven months in a horrendous fight for his country and for his life.

As we watched the Cobra flying above us, I went and stood beside him, and he told me the story of this Cobra.

When we saw that coming across the tree line, we knew we were getting out alive. —My Daddy.

The Cobra was a hybrid creation designed specifically for the Vietnam War, where the terrain made it almost impossible for air support. The fighting power and speed of a jet with the maneuvering and landing capabilities of a helicopter was needed. The Cobra went from drafting board to airborne in an astounding five months time. The pieces and parts were loaded onto aircraft carriers, assembled at sea, and then went straight from that flight deck to Viet Nam. Between 1967 and 1973, 1100 Cobra Attack Helicopters were produced, and they logged more than a million flight hours. The Cobra has impressive speeds of 165 mph and is equipped with armament, including a turret mounted on the front with miniguns and grenade launchers, wing-mounted pods with unguided missiles, and rockets. The minigun was a six-barrel rotary gun that could shoot 4000 rounds per minute. With two of those miniguns mounted on the front turret, that would be an astounding 8000 rounds per minute! The cannons, shot in tandem, had the capability of shooting six pairs of rockets per second. That's twelve rockets! Per second! When the Cobra designers labeled this an attack helicopter, they weren't playing. It was built for offense. Arriving early and staying late, it was designed to get our troops in and out alive.

In talking with my father about the Cobra Gunship, my understanding is that these gunships had two purposes. First, it would fly out in front of the troop-carrying Huey helicopters and clear the tree lines and fields of the enemy so that Huey could land and unload the troops safely. But what I saw in my daddy's eyes that day during Thunder Over Louisville was the second thing the Cobra did. It got them out alive. This was a war fought with boots on the ground, and typically, each battle would be won by whoever had the greatest number of troops in that particular fight. So when my daddy and his brothers in arms found themselves surrounded by enemy troops and all seemed lost, and that this actually could be their last fight, here it comes—the Cobra Gunship.

The Cobra could cover or "take out" the area of a football field with one pass. The miniguns' continuous ribbon of shells was not only accurate, but the incredibly rapid fire meant there were only inches between each shell. One fly by, one pass overhead could completely take out the enemy. Imagine the moment. Laying on the ground, trying to stay out of the crossfire coming in from all sides. You hear the noise, the yelling, the confusion, the fear. Your wounded brothers are lying around you, medics working furiously to save their lives and stop the dying. Your mind is swirling, looking for some way to get through this thing, to find a way out, and nothing seems possible. The enemy is closing in faster and faster with one goal in mind, to kill you. Then, off in the distance, you hear that sound. That recognizable sound of the whirling blades you've come to know as victory. And coming into view just off the horizon... the shark teeth. The Cobra Gunship. A weapon of war so terrifying and powerful you thank God it is on your side. That gunship was coming in for you. To save you. To get you out. It has one mission, and that mission is saving your life.

As I write this chapter, our youngest son Matthew is right now on his way overseas for his second deployment. The first one was a nine-month deployment to Afghanistan. This time, it's six months somewhere in the Middle East. Deployments into war zones have got to be one of the hardest things to reconcile as a mother. When he left for Afghanistan, he video called us just before his plane was taking off. My husband Mike and I were walking in our church parking lot. It was Sunday, July 22, 2018. We said all the things. We reminded him of the prayers we were praying, of God's promises, and as usual, we never say "goodbye." I remember going home after church and sitting outside on my porch looking at the yellow ribbon I had just tied around the post, crying and hashing it out with God. I told Him that I needed a day. Just one day. One day to let myself feel everything. To cry. To release. To not have to pick myself up. Just one day to not be strong. Just one day. But tomorrow! Tomorrow, I will rise. Tomorrow I will wash my face. I will get back on my hill. Tomorrow, His mercies are new, and I will walk in that truth. And that's what I did. I gave myself one day. As a mom, sometimes we need that day to let go, again, and to surrender our children back up to the Lord. Laying them back in the hands of the One who created them, knowing they are much safer there than they could ever be with us. I knew that realistically it would be far too easy to stay in that sulking place of letting go yet again, but I was determined to limit my time there. I knew that to be effective, to be my son's covering and shield while he was gone, I had to get back up! Nobody can fight while wallowing in pity lying on the ground. (You can insert here the thought of a toddler rolling around on the floor pitching a fit. This is the thought that always comes to my mind when I allow myself a pity party, which always drives me back to my rightful standing).

One prayer that has been on my lips for as long as I can remember goes something like this:

> *He will go before you*
> *He will be your rear guard*
> *He will hem you in on all sides*
> *He will cover you top to bottom*
> *And surround you with his hedge of protection.*

I pulled this prayer straight from scripture, and I declare it over my boys whenever they are heading off somewhere. It could be to school. It could be across the globe. It doesn't matter. I send them with this prayer. Before Matthew left for Afghanistan, I had that prayer along with some heartfelt words of a mother engraved on a metal, credit card-sized plate that he could put in his wallet and carry with him throughout the deployment. Before he left the second time, I felt I needed to expound on that prayer and tell him exactly what I was declaring over him as he went. I felt the need to highlight one scripture in particular.

> *The angel of the Lord encamps around those who fear*
> *him, and he delivers them.*
>
> PSALM 34:7

Even though Matthew grew up hearing this scripture spoken and prayed over him, I felt that I needed to remind him of the Lord's angels. When most people think of angels, they picture the pretty, blonde-haired, blue-eyed, fair-skinned lady in a flowing white satin lacy gown, non-proportional delicate wings on her back that are far too small to ever let her fly, and a pretty halo shining over her head. She sometimes carries a harp or a candle. She is kind and gentle and soft and billowy like the clouds. Others sometimes see a fat baby that flutters about with a little bow and arrow and wearing a diaper. I am never sorry to crush these images when I get the opportunity to tell people about what an angel truly is.

Let's look at some scriptures to help bring these angels into focus.

The angel of the Lord found Hagar, near a spring in the desert; And he said "Hagar servant of Sarai, where have you come from, and where are you going?"

GENESIS 16:7-8

Then the Lord opened Balaam's eyes, and he saw the angel of the Lord standing in the road with his sword drawn.

NUMBERS 22:31

Then the woman went to her husband and told him, "A man of God came to me. He looked like an angel of God, very awesome."

JUDGES 13:6

Take a special note: the word *awesome* used here means "to fear" in Hebrew.

Mary was greatly troubled at his words and wondered what kind of greeting this might be. But the angel said to her, "Do not be afraid, Mary; you have found favor with God."

LUKE 1:29-30

Just then, an angel of the Lord stood before them, and the glory of the Lord shone around them, and they were terrified. But the angel said to them, "Do not be afraid. I bring you good news that will cause great joy for all people."

LUKE 2:9-10

What do we see in all these scriptures regarding the angels of the Lord? They are referred to as "he", they carry swords, and they are terrifying to behold. Why else would they say, "do not be afraid"? When we look at the original word usage in the Bible, "do not be afraid" actually means to put to flight, to terrify, frighten. In my imaginative replay of these scenes, I see the angels saying, "Calm down, quit screaming, stop running away and flailing about. If you'd just listen, I have something exciting to tell you."

Let's keep going and look at three more encounters. First, we will look at what these people might be seeing when the angels appear to them while reassuring them with the words "do not be afraid."

. . . and in the fire was what looked like four living creatures. In appearance, their form was that of a man, but each of them had four faces and four wings. Their legs were straight; their feet were like those of a calf and gleamed like burnished

bronze. Under their wings on their four sides, they had the

hands of a man. All four of them had faces and wings, and

their wings touched one another. Each one went straight

ahead; they did not turn as they moved. Their faces looked

like this; each of the four had a face of a man, and on the

right side each had the face of a lion, and on the left the face

of an ox; each also had the face of an eagle.

EZEKIEL 1:5-10

When the creatures moved, I heard the sound of their

wings, like the roar of rushing waters, like the voice of the

Almighty, like the tumult of an army.

EZEKIEL 1:24

You can read more in Ezekiel chapter one about these amazing creatures. They truly are fascinating, and this account from Ezekiel gives us insight into what the heavenly creatures look like. There is nothing like this on earth, and to have this land in my backyard and start talking to me, honestly, just might make me have to change my pants.

Daniel also has an account that will shed some light.

I looked up and there before me was a man dressed in linen,

with a belt of the finest gold around his waist. His body was

like beryl, his face like lighting, his eyes like flaming torches,

his arms, and legs like the gleam of burnished bronze, and his

voice like the sound of a multitude.

I, Daniel, was the only one who saw the vision; the men with me did not see it, but such terror overwhelmed them that they fled and hid themselves.

DANIEL 10:5-7

Do you see him? Again, the angel in this passage is referred to as a "he." He has a face like lightning, eyes like flaming torches, and a voice that sounds like a multitude. Now, I don't know how many a multitude is, but according to Merriam-Webster, it is "a great number of people ". The voice coming out of him sounded like a great number of people speaking at once. Come on! Let's be honest. If we had been there to hear and see that, we would most likely have the same response as the men who ran and hid. Except did you catch that? The men ran and hid *without* having seen him. The angel carried with him the power and might and presence of Heaven that changed the very atmosphere to the point the men could not stand in that place because the presence alone was too great.

Then he continued, "Do not be afraid, Daniel. Since the first day that you set your mind to gain understanding and to humble yourself before God, your words were heard, and I have come in response to them. But the prince of the Persian kingdom resisted me twenty-one days. Then Michael, one of the chief princes, came to help me because I was detained there with the king of Persia.

DANIEL 10:12-13

The angel of the Lord, with flaming eyes and a scary voice, is telling Daniel that from the moment he set his heart on the Lord, this angel was launched from Heaven on his behalf. Then when that angel is met with opposition from the enemy, God launches another angel, Michael! Michael is the one who is referred to as the archangel, or head angel, in the book of Jude and also the one called the great military commander of an army of angels found in Revelations 12. God isn't playing, ladies! When He sends these angels, and they launch into motion, He sends them to win.

I have one more passage to share with you before I bring this thing home and make my point.

When the servant of the man of God got up and went out early the next morning, an army with horses and chariots had surrounded the city. "Oh, my lord, what shall we do?" the servant asked. "Don't be afraid," the prophet answered. "Those who are with us are more than those who are with them." And Elisha prayed, "O Lord, open his eyes so he may see." Then the Lord opened the servant's eyes, and he looked and saw the hills full of horses and chariots of fire all around Elisha.

2 KINGS 6:15-17

Oh Lord, may you open our eyes to see! What the servant saw on the hills were God's angels encamped around them! Not just one hill, but hills. Plural. Just because we cannot see with our human eyes does not mean they are not there. When my son left on his first deployment, in order to find my feet, to get up and wash my face, I needed God to remind me of who was going, who was being sent with my son. To give me sight. To let me see what I was praying. To see that those who are with us are more than those who are with them. As I prayed out the words "angels encamp around him," I asked God to show me once again, to let me see them, to see the angels encamped around my son.

Sometimes they show themselves as men in the Bible, and sometimes they show themselves as heavenly creatures and hosts. They are amazing beings, that until I get to Heaven or until I get an earthy sighting, I will never fully understand. What I am sure they are not are pretty ladies or soft chubby babies. They don't play harps or gently carry candles, careful not to move too fast so that their flame does not go out. Whether they come as men or come as heavenly hosts, one thing is for sure. They are awesome. They are massive. They are warriors. They are suited for battle. When they move, they make a sound like crashing waves, like a tumult of an army. The Hebrew word tumult is used only twice in the Bible, in the passage above, Ezekiel 1:24, and in Jeremiah 11:16, where it talks of an army coming to desolate a people. A sound of an army on a march, fueled by God's will, direction, and purpose. A mighty rushing sound. My husband and I tried to capture what the "roar of rushing waters" might sound like. We were staying on the ocean during a vacation, and there was a rocky cliff the waves were crashing against. We stood outside and closed our eyes, and let that sound sit deep in our spirits. Ezekiel describes the sound of crashing waves as the sound of the wings of angels. We recorded it on our phones in order to play it back to remind us of those who are with us and with our sons. I realize that this is probably not the exact sound they make, but Ezekiel had to use human words and earthly likeness to give us a glimpse of what he was experiencing.

The very moment you set your heart towards Him and begin to call down Heaven for the safety of your children, there are angels being launched, and no weapon formed against your children shall prosper (Isaiah 54:17). Why? Because just like the Cobra Gunship that came through for my daddy, there are angels coming in for our children, and they aren't playing. All the armament of the Cobra, all its guns and missiles and rockets and ability, are *nothing* compared to the armament of these angels armed with the weaponry of Heaven. They are not man-made and held within the compounds and restrictions of human thinking and ability. They are armed and purposed from God's own hand to cover, to fight, to protect, and to win. They are a weapon of warfare so terrifying and powerful that you thank God they are on your side. Their very presence alone causes men to run and hide. With one pass, one stand, one strike, they can completely obliterate the enemy. Those angels have one purpose, one mission to complete, and that mission is our children. They are going ahead of them to clear the way, they are encamped around them while they are there, and they are getting them out safely.

The Holy Spirit prompted me to remind my son of this before he left on his second deployment. I know he knows about the angels. This wouldn't be the first time he's heard me speak of them. But maybe, like me, he just needed reminding of what he was taking with him. Whatever the reason God encouraged me to say, it doesn't really matter. That is between Matthew and God. All that matters is that I follow through.

This is what I wrote out and sent my son off on deployment with:

When I pray for the angels to encamp around you, they aren't cute cherubs. They are massive, they are terrifying, they are armed with all of Heaven's power, and they do not lose! This is how you will make it back safe to me. You are on the winning team.

He's on God's team, and God always wins. This is what goes with your children as well. There are angels encamping around them. These angels go before your children. They go beside them. They provide shelter and covering. They will be their rear guard. As the army folk says, "they got your six." Know that your children are not alone. God, Himself will make sure of that!

THOUGHTS

THOUGHTS

SQUISH

laughter & tears

beginnings

MATTHEW'S
SIGNED CONTRACT

SWEARING IN

ADAM LAUNCHING

MATTHEW + ADAM

COBRA CIRCA 1970

HUEY CIRCA 1970

DAD CIRCA 1970

GRANDPA'S FISHIN' POLE

"When we saw that coming across the tree line, we knew we were getting out alive.

—daddy

ME + MY BOYS ♥

AFAGHANISTAN

COMING INTO PORT

LINE SHACK

MOTHER'S BLESSING

home & away

the
purple door

THE CLIMB

THE SUMMIT

— MT. FUJI —

my loves

ADAM · LYNDZIE · MIKE · SHERRY · MADDY · MATTHEW

eight

MOTCHECKS & STANDARDS

I REMEMBER WHEN WE MET our boys at their basic training graduations, and for lack of a better term, they seemed broken. They were not working right. They were not the same boys that had left our home for military training. The boys we picked up on graduation day had been replaced with people we did not recognize. It was hard to watch. It was hard to see how quickly the military had undone who they were and replaced them with the conformity that is the military. On graduation day, one of our sons had a moment of panic when he left his coat in our car after being instructed not to leave it anywhere. He was so distraught over it; he didn't even want to go back to the car to get the coat for fear of being caught without it. So, my husband went and retrieved the coat for him, and we could visibly see a wave of relief wash over him as my husband handed him the coat. *What on earth??* This was so unlike him. They also were no longer showing any signs of emotion. You couldn't tell what they were feeling, even if it was an extreme emotion like anger. I remember my son being irate at a situation he found himself in a year into his military contract. The only thing that led me to ask if he was okay was seeing his fists clenching at his side. It was barely visible, but I also knew the son I had raised would be furious so I was looking for signs. Once I asked him, he remembered who he was with and that we were a safe place to let that emotion out and vent. Had I not asked, his default would be to push it down and suppress any and all emotion. They were almost robotic in how they moved and how they responded. This is how they had been expected to behave during their time in the military.

In the book of Numbers, God speaks to Moses and Aaron and gives them instruction on how each tribe is to move forward, set up camp, and be represented around the tent of meetings, which was the portable earthly dwelling place of Yahweh. Part of the instruction was that the four tribes would each carry their own standard -Their own banner or flag.

The Israelites are to set up their tents by divisions, each man in his own camp under his own standard.

NUMBERS 1:52

The Lord said to Moses and Aaron: "The Israelites are to camp around the Tent of Meetings some distance from it, each man under his standard with the banners of his family."

NUMBERS 2:2

Standard is derived from the Hebrew word *dagal*, which means to look or behold. As the tribe's standard was raised, either while stationary or while in movement, those belonging to that household or tribe would rally beneath it and hold firm to what it represented. God was establishing His standards over those tribes by assigning to them the things He'd have each of them represent.

This is a practice that has been carried out through the ages. We see different kingdoms, countries, states, and provinces, each having a standard, banner, or flag representing them. Even sports teams have flags. When we see a flag, we recognize that that piece of cloth stands for something to them. It means something to somebody. We know that it has been established by a group of people to be a representation of them. Maybe the colors signify something. Maybe there is actually writing on the flag. Pictures are common. People have flags and banners, and standards because it has meaning in an area of their life that is important to them.

If you ask me what my favorite color is, I will always tell you it's rainbow. I love rainbows. I have all sorts of rainbow apparel, shoes, shirts, even eyeglasses because to me, the rainbow is a standard I want to represent and raise over my own life. The rainbow is a banner that God painted in the sky as a promise from Himself to Noah. When I behold the sky painted with the banner of the rainbow after a storm, I am reminded of how God's promises are true. The banner that was given to Noah as a promise still shows itself today, all these many years later, which proves to me that He is a God of yesterday, today, and tomorrow. I believe in His promises. That is what the standard of the rainbow is for me.

I am also a big lover of the Red, White, and Blue. I have American flags of all ages displayed around my home. I have one in my car tucked into the air vent that waves when the air is on. We fly one from a pole in our yard, both outside our business and outside our home. I have American flag boots, shirts, and jewelry. Why? Because I believe in the standards this country was founded on. I believe in One Nation Under God. I believe in this nation and in the men and women that have and will always defend her. It's a standard I'm proud to represent.

It is with these principles and ideas in mind that Mike and I knew we wanted to establish our own standard as a family. We don't have a physical flag that we have designed and sewn and subsequently fly outside our home. We don't wear it. It doesn't sit on a shelf. It's not a physical standard, but rather a spiritual one. Together as we serve the Lord, He has planted in our hearts His truths to strive to live upright lives that would reflect Him well. This became the standard we built the foundation of our family on. When the boys were growing up, we called this banner "Remember, you're a Motcheck." We would say those words anytime we wanted them to remember that their behavior was representing us as a family. We said it to them as they would leave the house, knowing full well they had a clear understanding of what that meant. We, as a God-established family of four, together and independently have the opportunity to represent Him well, to be His ambassadors and regents while raising the standard He established over our household.

Here are some of the behavioral standards or truths our banner "Remember you're a Motcheck" represents.

» Put God first. Every time.

As for me and my household, we will serve the Lord (Joshua 24:15).

» Your word means something; don't give it if you aren't going to stand behind it. When you shake someone's hand, make it firm, look them in the eye, and know it is the same as signing a contract.

Do not break your oath. . . (Matthew 5:33).

Simply let your 'Yes' be 'Yes," and your 'No' be 'No'
(Matthew 5:37).

» If your neighbor is in need and you can help, you best be helping.

"The King will reply, 'I tell you the truth, whatever you did
for one of the least of these brothers of mine, you did for
me' (Matthew 25:35-40 vs 40).

» Character and integrity are tested best when no one is looking; just because no one sees it, don't think it won't matter because you'll know, and God will know.

There is nothing concealed that will not be disclosed or
hidden that will not be made known (Matthew 10:26).

» Your reputation is fragile. Don't take it for granted; it's hard to build it back up.

May integrity and uprightness protect me because my
hope is in you (Psalm 25:21).

» You will be held accountable for your actions. If you do wrong, make it right.

So then, each of us will give an account of himself to God
(Romans 14:12).

» Always do the honorable thing.

To those who, by persistence in doing good, seek
glory, honor, and immortality, he will give eternal life
(Romans 2:7).

» Be humble in your wins and gracious in your losses; no one likes a bragger or a sore loser.

The reward for humility and fear of the Lord is riches and
honor in life (Proverbs 22:4).

Pride goes before destruction, a haughty spirit before a
fall (Proverbs 16:18).

» If you fall down, rub some dirt on it and get back up. You got this!

. . . but those who hope in the Lord will renew their
strength. They will soar on wings like eagles; they will
run and not grow weary; they will walk and not be faint
(Isaiah 40:31).

» Be a leader and not a follower.

The Lord will make you the head, not the tail. If you
pay attention to the commands of the Lord your God
that I give you this day and carefully follow them,
you will always be at the top and not the bottom
(Deuteronomy 28:13).

» Always shine bright.

You are the light of the world. A city on a hill cannot be
hidden (Matthew 5:14).

» Make wise choices

She [wisdom] is more precious than rubies; nothing you
desire can compare to her (Proverbs 3:15).

These were words we spoke over our boys while they were growing up. It's how they were raised. These behavioral standards were nonnegotiable. They were collectively a bar and expectation we set as a couple and as parents. This is who we are and how we will conduct ourselves. We are the Motchecks, and this is how we will be known. All of these standards are based on the scriptures God placed in our hearts. We wanted them woven into the fabric of our family, into the spiritual banner God was creating in us and for us. We want to be a family that represents Him well. When we raise our standard, and we rally beneath it, we want everyone to behold it and see Him being raised.

There are other truths we instilled in our sons, some of which you will find in other areas of this book. Promises and blessings of God and gifts of Heaven we pull down over our children and even over our children's children who are not yet here on earth. This chapter focuses on how we will conduct ourselves. Our behaviors. Who we wanted our boys to be as people. We wanted to instill and sow godly character into them, establishing the truths that when woven together make up the Motcheck standard.

After joining the military, the Motcheck banner still flies over our sons. These declarations cover them everywhere they go. Being part of something as big as the military has a way of changing and forming them into something they were not before they joined. But the new person they are becoming in serving our country is layered or built *on top* of what God had already established in them as young men of the Lord.

I have often witnessed how mothers tend to take a step back and stop raising the family banner over their children as they leave home. It is sometimes hard to know where and when you may still have a voice in your child's life. We spend eighteen-plus years pouring into them and then pray and hope we've done enough for them to stand on their own once they leave. We want them to be independent, adult children leading their own lives and the lives of their families. So, our tendency is to step back, lift our hands from them and watch and hope we've given them enough to succeed. Sometimes it's a tough transition while they make this move to adulthood. Boys will test their fathers, and daughters will challenge their mothers as they try to become the man or woman making their own choices. During this process, children can sometimes wobble and teeter and get tossed around as they try and find their new footing. Sadly, you may find your children doing the very thing you taught them not to do. These people we are seeing our children become are not who we raised them to be. Don't let your eyes trick your spirit into seeing something that is not real. This is a spiritual optical illusion put in front of us by the enemy.

I believe sometimes God lets us *not* see the true reality with our natural eyes because He is wanting us to see with our spiritual eyes. Unlike our human, made of flesh eyes, our spiritual eyes can see what God sees. There is a whole other realm out there that is more real than our earthly realm, but we cannot see it with the eyes of our flesh. This is similar to the stereogram visual images that were a big hit in the '90s, where it looks like just a bunch of repetitive colors and shapes that really have no apparent rhyme or reason, but if you get really still, and focus really hard, all of sudden something starts to emerge. You catch something, something that may be something, and then it leaves again and you are back to looking at the randomness that you started with. But, surely you saw something. There *was* something there, and determination to see this something in its completeness sets it. You got a glimpse of it once, and so you won't stop until you see the fullness. It seems the harder you focus, the more the image fades away. But, if you just let the image come to you, something shifts. Suddenly, out of the flat image of random colors and patterns springs forth an image of a horse running with his tail and mane flying in the wind with so much dimension it's as if you could reach right into that photo and pick it up. It's mind-blowing. It is something that makes zero sense to our eyes and our brains. That is what seeing the things of the Kingdom can feel like here on earth. We need to learn to flip the enemy's optical illusions around and let him know that no matter what we "see" with our flesh eyes, it is not what we see with our spiritual eyes, and he's not fooling anybody. Your child may look like they are in the midst of producing a bunch of repetitive nonsense that is not fitting of who you raised them to be. Don't fret! God is not finished with your child yet! There is still a deep work being done in your child's life. You need to get back to what you know, what He showed you in your secret place, what He will continue to reveal to you as you learn to pull out the godly qualities, character, and destiny from that image your child is projecting that looks like chaos and confusion.

As a parent, you just want to fix them and make the nonsense stop. There is part of you that wants to shake them and ask, "Are you still in there somewhere? What is happening?" This is just one of the things you may encounter where you see things that do not align with what you know them to be. There are many other behaviors and choices that, at the onset, try to rattle you. Just remember, this is not who they are and what you are seeing is not what you know. What you know is that God has brought them to the military, and He gets the last say! If we don't get hung up on trusting our eyes, and instead we learn to trust God, we will watch as our newly broken child is replaced with who they were born to become in the military. Just like in that three-dimensional image, keep looking past what it seems to be, and who they truly are will come into view. They will find their way back to who God created them to be. I believe there is a work being done in them, even as we see them "broken," and something is being established for the Kingdom even while it seems it is far from that in the moment. Both of my boys have since found their way through the brokenness and have been "repaired." Hang in there. It might take a minute for that reboot to happen, but happen it will. Don't lose your footing or get discouraged. They will come back around.

For now we see only a reflection as in a mirror; then we shall see face to face. Now I know in part; then I shall know fully, even as I am fully known.

1 CORINTHIANS 13:12

We will always only know in part until we see God face to face. He will never reveal His full and total picture or plan with us; the humanity part of us would not be able to handle that much information. We are only responsible for what He does reveal to us. The more time we spend longing and searching into the things of Heaven, the more it comes into view. Wouldn't it be amazing to get a glimpse into Heaven as John does in the book of Revelations? Let's press in for that. If it happened once, it can happen again. Let's determine to make sure we are "seeing" the Kingdom's realities and not settling for the illusions of earth.

When it looks bleak, you start reclaiming the ground you may have found yourself no longer defending. Maybe you've stepped back, just for a moment, believing your work was done and it no longer bears witness in their lives. It isn't, and it does! Don't lose hope. Don't count it all as a loss. Don't believe the lie that your prayers, your covering, and your banners are no longer effective now that your children are out of your house. Your anointing and authority to pull those banners and coverings over your children remain no matter where they are.

If you have ever been to a large stadium during a sporting event and watched several people grab ahold of an American Flag and unfurl it out over the field as the National Anthem plays, there is nothing quite like it. I witnessed it myself at an NFL football game years ago. Folks line up in the center of the field from end zone to end zone in two long rows facing each other. A massive flag which has been strategically rolled into a tube lays in their hands. As the anthem begins to play, the flag handlers grab the edges of that flag and run in opposite directions, each row running towards the sideline nearest them, reaching to the outermost edges of that field until that flag is unfurled and opened in all of its glory, covering that field edge to edge. Extra folks come running out and join in to grab hold of the ends so that the flag never touches the ground. Seeing that flag displayed across that field is a moment to reflect on what a great country this is and how we all are so incredibly blessed to live here. As an American, I can imagine each of us being tucked beneath that flag as it unfurls out over our heads, held by the men and women who have

"

When it looks bleak,

start reclaiming

the ground

you may have found

yourself no longer

defending.

————————

and still are fighting to defend our freedoms that make this country so great. When you couple that with having your son or daughter as being one of those that defend that amazing flag, wow! What a powerful moment. This act of unfurling a flag on a ball field also gives an amazing heavenly picture for our lives. As believers, we are tucked beneath an even greater canopy, one which God has unfurled above us.

He sits enthroned above the circle of the earth, and its people are like grasshoppers. He stretches out the heavens like a canopy and spreads them out like a tent to live in.

ISAIAH 40:22B

God unfurls all of Heaven over us; His canopy is stretched out over us like a tent in which to live. When the standards were first introduced in the Bible, there was a tabernacle, a dwelling place of God, that was portable and could be moved about the earth. When Jesus came, He did away with the old things and made something new. He made *us* God's dwelling place. We are now His temple.

Don't you know that you yourselves are God's temple and that God's Spirit dwells in your midst?

1 CORITHIANS 3:16

Wherever we go, His temple goes, and His canopy covers us. I envision that canopy rippling overhead caused by the breath of the Spirit and the movement of angel wings as they launched into action on our behalf.

Sometimes I stand still when a breeze blows over me. I close my eyes, and I imagine that the breeze is caused by God's canopy over me responding to the movement going on in Heaven. I am being kissed by the breeze it creates. Only He knows where it started, and only He knows where it will end. I am blessed to have been in its path. He is an infinite God. He is alive and active, Heaven is unfurled above us, and we have been chosen to represent it in all its glory.

The wind blows wherever it pleases. You hear its sound, but you cannot tell where it comes from or where it is going. So it is with everyone born of the spirit.

JOHN 3:8

Joining the military comes with deep respect and honor of the United States Flag and a fierceness to protect it. The flag represents the freedom and attributes of the very things that caused our sons and daughters to join the military in the first place. There are codes of honor and creeds the different branches are made to memorize, and more importantly, they are taught to live their lives by it. It starts when they are sworn into the military, and it continues on from there. When our son graduated from Army basic training, all the graduates marched out onto a field. The field had smoke flares lit for dramatic effect as the graduates came marching in through the thick haze towards us. They had AC/DC's song Thunderstruck blaring on the speakers. As they made their way to our side of the field, they came to a halt. All went quiet as the graduates stood in impressive formation in front of the bleacher-style stands where those attending the graduation were seated. Then in unison, they all recited the Soldiers Creed.

I am an American Soldier.

I am a warrior and a member of a team.

I serve the people of the United States and live the Army
*   Values*

I will always place the mission first.

I will never accept defeat.

I will never quit.

I will never leave a fallen comrade.

I am disciplined, physically and mentally tough, trained,
*   and proficient in my warrior tasks and drills.*

I will always maintain my arms, my equipment, and
*   myself.*

I am an expert, and I am a professional.

I stand ready to deploy, engage and destroy the enemies of
*   the United States in close combat.*

I am a guardian of freedom and the American way of life.

I am an American Soldier.

The last line was shouted louder than the rest, and the stands went wild with applause and cheers. It was a proud moment; they'd made it through basic training. It was also a moment that brought the declarations my son was speaking over his own life to my attention. From this point on, every time he saw Old Glory flying, it would never again be just our nation's flag. From now on, when he looks at the flag, everything he just spoke out on that field, he will see waving through those colors of red, white, and blue. The Marines have the saying Semper Fidelis, Latin for always faithful. The Navy has a Sailors Creed. The Air Force has a Creed, the Coast Guard has a creed, and even the military academy has a Cadet Honor Code that reads, "A cadet won't lie, cheat or steal or tolerate those who do." This is just the tip of the iceberg of military sayings, mottos, and words to live by. There are hundreds more centered around this amazing country, the flag that represents it, and the men and women serving to defend her. What am I trying to say? I'm trying to help correlate how a banner- in this case, the United States Flag- can bring about or even command a certain behavior that can be forever life-changing.

If you haven't witnessed that fierce respect, honor, and protection of our flag with your child yet, you will. The first time I witnessed it was when we were visiting the Naval base in Japan. We were walking with our son as "Retreat" and "To the Colors" started playing over the PA system. As the first notes were played out, the world on that base literally stopped turning. Cars stopped right where they were on the road. Every man, woman, and child outdoors stopped in their tracks and turned towards the flag standing at attention. It was something that took us off guard the first time it happened. We looked around as if we were seeing something out of another world. It was almost apocalyptic. To see something command that level of respect was stunning, to say the least. As the days rolled out, though, we too became accustomed to expecting it every afternoon and joined in with those on the base standing unmoving while the song played over the PA. There on that base, seeing the respect of the flag built new respect in us. I have also witnessed our sons right a flag on its pole, almost unconsciously as they walk past one the wind has caused it to spin out of alignment. They straighten lapel pins on my jackets. They refold flags I have stored on a shelf. Anything that causes that flag to not be displayed at its best, protected, and honored, they will remedy.

So, let me pitch you this. If in such a short amount of time our children are taught to honor and revere an earthly flag at such a degree that they will stop in their tracks as it is raised and lowered, that seeing one wrapped around a pole by the wind makes them stop what they are doing to straighten it, that what they have had built in them by the military stays with them for life, how much more should they be taught about the awesome canopy of Heaven that is stretched out and unfurled above them? If being in the military brings about certain behavior to ensure they are representing the best of the Red White and Blue, being a son and daughter of the most high King should warrant certain behavior as well, bringing about the best representation of Him. In so doing, they can represent the Kingdom well and who they were born to be well. We bring awareness of that to them by ringing the bells of Heaven's freedom over them, by speaking godly attributes over them, by raising a banner over them, and by declaring those things that that banner represents over them. In time, they will understand that pulling their corner of this nation's flag over this country and defending the freedoms it brings to all Americans *pales* in comparison with the power and freedom the canopy of Heaven that God has stretched out above them brings!

It doesn't matter if they know we are praying. It doesn't matter where they are or what they are doing. None of that matters when God is in control. When you hold fast and continue to declare the truth of who they are over your kids, Heaven will handle the rest. Until they are able to do it themselves, we do it for them. We grab a corner of Heaven's canopy and start running towards them, and then Heaven unfurls above them, and Kingdom truth kicks out the lies they may be wading through. You will see them begin to think differently, walk differently, and believe differently as they start to carry the attributes of Heaven. The things that are not of Him will begin to fade away, and His character will begin to shine through in who they are and what they do. They are made in His image, and they were born to reflect Him and to carry the traits of the Father.

The difference between the American flag and the canopy of God is God's canopy doesn't just cover a stadium from edge to edge. It covers to the very ends of the earth. There is nowhere your sons and daughters can go where they do not stand beneath it. Don't let the discouraging moment you may be looking at become bigger than that truth. Your family banner and standards still cover your children. The prayers you have prayed over them all these years still count. They still hold true. They don't go void. They don't come back unanswered. Just as His Kingdom never passes away, neither will the things *of* His Kingdom pass away.

His dominion is an everlasting dominion that will not pass away, and his kingdom is one that will never be destroyed.

DANIEL 7:14

Pray it out, mamas! Be bold. Don't be afraid to clear the dust from the air for them from time to time so they can clearly see God and His canopy overhead. Remind them of the canopy of Heaven they are standing under. Remind them who they are and to whom they belong. They are sons and daughters of the most high King, and they need to act like it. His promises and truths over their lives still stand. No matter what influence Uncle Sam may have in their lives, there is a banner of God emblazoned on them that cannot be removed or taken down in Jesus' Name.

Now, you might be thinking that you really missed the boat on this because you never did this with your kids growing up. You may have never really set up standards like this. Well, here's the good news. We serve a God outside of time and space. His time is not linear like ours is. He can speed time up. He can slow time down. There is no space or distance when it comes to what God can do. He is a God that always was, always has been, and always will be for you and for your children. It's never too late. Start today! Start setting up a banner over your family, over your sons, over your daughters. Begin to declare truths over them, unfurl the canopy of Heaven's promises over them. Whatever years you feel like you have lost or missed your chance on, He will give them back.

The Lord says, "I will repay you for the years the locusts have eaten."

JOEL 2:25

What are the things you want for your children? If you could hand something to your children for them to live under as covering all their days on earth which will prepare them for eternity, what would that be? Start declaring those things. Make a list. What are the things of character and integrity you want your children to carry? If they are attributes of God, He has already made a way for them to walk in those through the work of His Son on the Cross. Victory is already theirs; you just need to start declaring it.

The very fact that you have the children you have is His promise over your life that you were designed and equipped to be a mother. The very fact those children are now in the military means He trusted you to raise a warrior. You couldn't have raised a warrior if there wasn't a warrior in you! You are stronger than you know. You are the one He chose to be the mother of your son or your daughter. You are the only one equipped with this specific anointing over your children. No one else will have the anointing of a mother that God has given you for your children. When you feel small and unable, who do you think is telling you that? That will never come from God's heart. Don't listen to it. Rise up, take your place, and begin to war for your children and declare godly attributes over them. Speak out the behavior that being Heaven's Royalty brings with it. Those are the things we are calling forth in our children. Remember, you are in the exact place and anointing He designed for you. Declare with authority. Declare with expectation. Declare knowing He will move time and space to make His Kingdom come in the lives of your children. Start today!

There is a banner of Heaven raised over our children, and it is flying from God's mighty hand. Whatever feeling rises up within them when they see our nation's flag flying is nothing to what they are going to feel when they see God's canopy waving overhead! Let it be so! In Jesus' Name!

THOUGHTS

THOUGHTS

nine

INHERITANCE & GENERATIONS

SEVERAL YEARS AGO, when I was cautiously stepping out and working towards becoming a pastor, I was nervously preparing a message on being a fisher of men. God had woken me up one morning and said, "If you want to be a fisher of men, there are some important things you will need in your tackle box." This message was about that tackle. I was new and green and felt completely unqualified to be a deliverer of God's words to the masses. One day, I just felt led to talk to my dad about this message, how it was coming together, and how small I felt. He listened and then stood up and said, "Come out here a minute. I have something for you." I followed him outside and into his garage. He rummaged around a bit and then pulled out an old fishing pole. It was apparent it had some years on it. I could see the chrome reel had some rust speckled about. The off-white and brown paint on the pole itself had some cracks, and the decals were pulling away in some places. The line was loose and brittle. This fishing pole had some history. As he handed it to me, he said, "This was my dad's, and I want you to have it." As I held that pole in my hands, I felt like I was holding the most valuable thing on earth. My grandfather, an amazing man of faith, had passed away and gone on to glory twenty-five years prior when I was twelve years old. This was one of the treasures my dad had inherited. It may have seemed like just an old fishing pole to others, but I knew it was precious to my dad, and because of that, it is also precious to me. But this gift is also bigger than being an heirloom. God had set this into motion long before this moment. He knew that down my grandfather's line, a granddaughter would arise, and when she felt a little wobbly on her feet as she walked the direction God was leading, this pole would stand her back up straight. My dad gave me this fishing pole to empower me to preach a message that I was born to share about being a fisher of men. I took that pole home and hung it on the wall in our family room, where it still hangs today. When I see it up on our wall, I am reminded that this is a gift from my dad that showed me how proud he was of me, and in that moment, he saw more in me than I saw in myself. This wasn't just my grandfather's fishing pole. I believe God knew that pole had to get from my grandfather to my father and onto me. My grandfather never got to see me become a pastor or hear me give that message. He never got to see the impact his fishing pole has had on my life, but I know that I am walking in the fruit from his life serving the Lord. His walk with the Lord helped to point me to where I stand today.

God has always been multigenerational. He is never doing something with one generation that He hasn't planned for with the generations before as well as the generations that will follow. Where you are standing right now has been influenced by your parents, grandparents, great-grandparents, and so on. Where you stand now will also have an impact on the generations that follow you. While God's timeline is not linear, the way we as humans see Him move is. Things carry forward into the next generation from those who have gone before us. In our Bibles, we see examples of God doing that. He reaches into the life of someone, raises them to their rightful standing, and protects them because somewhere down their family tree, others are meant to do something extraordinary too!

Rahab comes to mind. Rahab comes on the scene in Joshua chapter two. Joshua sends two spies out to scout the city of Jericho. When the king of Jericho finds out there are spies in his city, he sets out to find them. But Rahab hides the spies in her roof thatching to keep them safe.

Before the spies lay down for the night, she went up on the roof and said to them, "I know that the Lord has given this land to you and that a great fear of you has fallen on us, so that all who live in this country are melting in fear because of you. We have heard how the Lord dried up the water of the Red Sea for you when you came out of Egypt. ...When we heard of it, our heart melted, and everyone's courage failed because of you, for the Lord your God is God in heaven above and on the earth below.

JOSHUA 2:8-10, 11B

Why would Rahab hide the spies if she knew they were coming to destroy her city? Because she knew they served the one true God! The God in Heaven above and on earth below. If anyone could keep her safe during the upcoming invasion, the one true God could, and the men she was hiding in her roof thatching were God's ambassadors! Surely if she shows favor to God's men, He would have mercy on her. So she asks the spies that in return for her keeping them hidden and safe, they would show kindness and spare the lives of her family and all those belonging to them when they come back to take the city. The men agree and tell her to put everyone, her father and mother, brothers and sister, and all who belong to them inside her house and to tie a scarlet cord in the window as a sign to the invading army that her household would not be touched.

This is a great example of when we see God being multigenerational. Rahab was standing in a heaven-colliding-with-earth moment. Her declaration about who God is and her bold actions that follow saved not only herself but the generation behind her (her mother and father), her current generation (her brothers and sisters), *and* the generations yet to come from her line. Rahab goes on to marry Salmon from the tribe of Judah, and from her comes a son Boaz, and from Boaz comes a son named Obed, from Obed comes a son named Jesse, and from Jesse comes a son named David who will grow to become king, and from the line of King David, comes our Savior, Jesus Christ. God needed to keep Rahab safe because she was meant to significantly impact the generations around her and the generations yet to come. Rahab would never live to meet David, but her walk with God impacted him becoming a king! I don't know about you, but this gets my heart beating with excitement! It makes me wonder what God has planned for the people down my generational line that I am impacting right now in my walk with him today.

We also see many places in scripture, both in the Old Testament and in the new, the reference to Abraham, Isaac, and Jacob. These three men represent three generations. They are known as the patriarchs. Abraham is the father of Isaac, and Isaac is the father of Jacob. The mention of these three names together by Jesus in the book of Matthew is God showing us in scripture how important generations and legacy are. Jesus is pulling an Old Testament passage from Exodus 3:6 and reciting it so that it now lives in the New Testament in red letters!

I am the God of Abraham, the God of Isaac, and the
God of Jacob.

MATTHEW 22:32

God gave Abraham a promise for him and the generations that would follow him. We are descendants of Abraham, and what he did as a man of faith reverberated down through the generations after him and is still impacting us today. God used Abraham to start the process of generational inheritance.

All the land that you see I will give to you and your
offspring forever.

GENESIS 13:15

No longer will you be called Abram; your name will be Abraham,
for I have made you a father of many nations. I will make
you very fruitful; I will make nations of you, and kings will
come from you. I will establish my covenant as an everlasting
covenant between me and you and your descendants after you
for the generations to come, to be your God and the God of
your descendants after you.

GENESIS 17:5

An everlasting covenant means it never stops. It's a continuous out-pouring of promise that we are still walking in today.

You are all sons of God through faith in Christ Jesus, for all
of you who were baptized into Christ have clothed yourselves
with Christ. There is neither Jew nor Greek, slave nor free,
male nor female, for you all are one in Christ Jesus. If you
belong to Christ, then you are Abraham's seed and heirs
according to the promise.

GALATIANS 3:26-29

Not only are we descendants of Abraham and walking in *his* inheritance, but we are also God's children walking in Heaven's inheritance.

The Spirit himself testifies with our spirit that we are
God's children. Now, if we are children, then we are heirs-
heirs of God and co-heirs with Christ if indeed we share in
his sufferings in order that we may also share in his glory.

ROMANS 8:16-17

The Spirit (with a capital S) is the Holy Spirit. He is testifying or telling our spirit (with a lower-case s) that we are joint-heirs with Jesus Christ, God's only begotten Son. This is big, y'all. This is saying that everything God the Father gave His Son as an inheritance is ours too! Jesus made a way for us to have a heavenly inheritance, and through the work of the Cross, He is saying to us, "This is my Dad's, and I want you to have it."

Part of what we know as the Lord's Prayer is, "*Thy Kingdom come, thy will be done, on earth as it is in heaven.*" Now, let's just think about this for a second. Jesus was using this prayer to teach his disciples how to pray. Jesus wouldn't tell them to pray something or declare something that wouldn't be true or wouldn't work. On earth, as it is in Heaven, is ours to walk in. It's an inheritance of a holy collision of Heaven meeting earth over our lives. Whatever is going on in Heaven is ours to have on earth! All we have to do is ask God what is going on up there and then pull that down as our inheritance. That is so powerful.

A good man leaves an inheritance for his children's children.

PROVERBS 13:22

I believe that this is true both monetarily and also spiritually. My husband and I have been sticking money away for our children's children who aren't even on this earth yet because we believe that legacy and inheritance is more powerful than we will ever understand on this side of Heaven. But even more important than financial inheritance, we want to impact the generations coming after us with Kingdom inheritance. That is a legacy that moths and rust cannot destroy.

Do not store up for yourselves treasure on earth, where moth and rust destroy, and where thieves break in and steal. But store up for yourselves treasure in heaven, where moth and rust do not destroy, and where thieves do not break in and steal. For where your treasure is, there your heart will be also.

MATTHEW 6:19-24

There are times as I settle myself into His presence, I close my eyes, and I can see in the spirit a massive vault in Heaven. It has the big thick door with the spoked- spinney handle you'd see at a bank. But because this is my inheritance, that door is wide open to me. The vault stretches as far as my eyes can see into the distance. There are so many things in this vault, and everything in there is what God wants for His children to have. Things I have yet to discover. More things than I ever *will* discover on this side of Heaven. I just see Him smiling and saying, "Baby girl, everything in here is yours. Just go in and get it." Like my earthly father did with the fishing pole, my heavenly Father wants to pass me things as well. Things that build me, shape me, prepare me, empower me, and make me more like Him. Everything I could ever need is in that vault. Whatever we can carry out from that vault becomes a Kingdom inheritance for our children and our children's children.

There is fruit that will come out from our lives that will feed the generations coming behind us. You can see this Kingdom promise work even if the generations that follow aren't yet believers. I have watched good people who do not know Jesus Christ as their personal Savior not only walk in Kingdom blessing, but they give out Kingdom blessing to others around them without even knowing that is what they are doing. An unsaved neighbor who is compelled to shovel the walk of the widow next door is fruit coming straight out of James 1:27. Wealthy folks compelled to give money to a missionary who is starting a Christian school in a third world country is a fruit to further the Great Commission, even if the wealthy folk doesn't know what that is. Kingdom principles work even when those walking them out don't realize it. All you have to do is look back in the lineage of that unsaved person, and you will find there was someone in the generations before them who loved the Lord, walked in His blessings, and pulled down the inheritance of Heaven. It is from the seed of that fruit that the new fruit is starting to grow. The unsaved neighbor mostly likely had a father or grandfather who modeled acts of godly service and compassion, and now that rings in the unsaved neighbors' spirit too. Now his desire is to share and give out that same fruit he inherited. The wealthy folks probably had parents or grandparents that believed in the Great Commission and gave faithfully to missions. Now they also carry the fruit for missions. That Kingdom inheritance passes down because God is a multigenerational God.

There is a term called old money. It describes a social class of rich people who have been able to maintain their wealth for many generations. The ones who currently hold the wealth may not even know who or how it got started in the first place. All they know is they have money in the bank that they didn't work for or earn. Listen, if it works with earthly money, how much more will it work with Kingdom inheritance and blessing? All we have to do is get into that vault and take it so that we can pass it on.

Right before the children of Israel were exiled from Egypt, God gave them their rightful inheritance.

And I will make the Egyptians favorably disposed toward this people so that when you leave, you will not go empty handed. Every woman is to ask her neighbor and any woman living in her house for articles of silver and gold and for clothing, which you will put on your sons and daughters.

EXODUS 3:21-22

The Egyptians, the enemy, the *slave owners* just open handedly gave up the goods to the women they enslaved! That's just hard to get my head around. Then after receiving the goods, the women strapped those goods on their children, and the children carried off the spoils of war. They had been enslaved for 400 years. That is four generations' worth of loot those children carried out. Not only that, Exodus 12:37 says there were 600,000 men plus women, children, and livestock. These sons and daughters carried out enough goods to sustain that many people! I would also pitch out there that it was from these spoils they were able to create the brazen altar and provide every detailed gold, silver, and bronze item needed for the tabernacle. They had the jewels needed for the ephods and the blue and purple and scarlet yarns needed for the courtyard curtains. That's quite an inheritance! It was always God's intention to take care of His children. If the enemy has taken something from them that was God's intended inheritance, the enemy has to give it back. There was no fight or battle; it was simply handed over.

God will restore to you and your family line things He never took away. Things the enemy took. Things we laid down. Things we just never bothered to pick up. The things that are rightfully yours and mine, as heirs of the King, He will restore to us. One of those things is salvation. If your child doesn't walk with the Lord, call him or her back to rightful standing! That is their inheritance. The most important thing God wants His children to have is a relationship with His Son. It's never too late to see them come to know Jesus or to get to where they once were if they've stumbled away.

"

The most important
thing God wants
His children to have
is a relationship
with His Son.
it's never too late...

———————

I will repay you for the years the locusts have eaten.

JOEL 2:25

I have referenced this passage in Joel previously in this book, but I just want you to reread it. You may be looking at years of your child running the other way. Remember God is a God outside of time and space, and He can restore what the enemy has taken. Not only can He bring your child back to right standing with Jesus, but then your child will be showered with the blessings stored up for him or her. The enemy has to hand them over. Remember Abraham? The one we are a descendant of? The blessings our children will reap start from there.

When the Lord your God brings you into the land he swore to your fathers, to Abraham, Isaac and Jacob, to give you- a land with large, flourishing cities you did not build, houses filled with all kinds of good things you did not provide, wells you did not dig, and vineyards and olive groves you did not plant-then when you eat and are satisfied, be careful that you do not forget the Lord.

DEUTERONOMY 6:10-12

There were wells dug by the generations before me that I now drink from. There were vineyards planted far before I came on the scene, but now I'm getting to be part of that harvest. My grandmother was an amazing woman of faith. I know it is partly because of the fields she tilled before

I ever came to be that I stand in the place of harvest I do today. I am walking in the legacy and inheritance and fruit of her dedicated life with Jesus. One of my earthly treasures is my grandfather's Bible, the same grandfather whose fishing pole hangs on my wall. I can leaf through his Bible and see the wells and vineyards he planted far before my time in the markings he left on the pages. I walk in his inheritance.

Part of Isaac's story is about a time he went to reclaim the wells his father had dug.

So Isaac moved away from there and encamped in the Valley of Gerar and settled there. Isaac reopened the wells that had been dug in the time of this father Abraham, which the Philistines had stopped up after Abraham died.

GENESIS 26:17-18

After Abraham died, the enemy had filled in the wells with dirt, trying to stop the blessing from reaching the next generation. But Isaac knew the wells were there and that if he removed all the garbage the enemy had used to try and stop it up, water would flow. It's time for us to start uncovering the blessings the generations before us have dug.

What does this look like practically to live a life that leaves a legacy? I think it comes from the last few words of Deuteronomy 6:12, "be careful that you do not forget the Lord." Every financial blessing in my life, I point back to God. Every good thing that ever happens, I point it back to God. Every healing, every job, every wise decision, every earthly good, everything restored, everything that brought me favor, everything

He has torn down or built back up, every door opened, and every door closed, I point back to Him. Every time I am broken, hurt, or lost, I still point back to Him. He is the point I start from and the place I will always point back to.

Every good and perfect gift is from above, coming down from the Father of the heavenly lights, who does not change like shifting shadows.

JAMES 1:17

The healing, favor, restoration, wisdom, prosperity, open doors, shut doors that I mentioned above, those are all blessings or gifts that I got out of the vault. Because they are now mine, I can pass those on to my heirs; My children and my children's children. I do it through prayer. I do it through declarations. I do it through teachable moments and in conversations where I plant seeds in the good soil of their hearts. They will walk in it because I have claimed it. I believe there are dreams God has planted in my heart that will not be mine to walk in, but dreams I am tilling the ground for generations behind me to walk in. David had a dream of building a temple, a dwelling for the Ark of the Covenant to reside. However, it was not David that God wanted to fulfill that dream but his son Solomon that would build the temple. You may have dreams God will fulfill through your children!

Everything in this book up to now has hopefully inspired you to reach further into the vault of promises and blessings God has for you and your children. Hopefully, you are becoming stronger, braver, and more fierce as

a warrior and shield-maiden of Heaven. Hopefully, you have been empowered to rise and be counted as the hero of Heaven I know you are meant to
be as you war for our country and our children. But I want to encourage
you to push farther. Push beyond your children and those presently in your
life. I want you to war for the generations that will follow them, even for
the ones you may never meet. You have been called to this position for a
greater purpose than you may never know or see while you are here on
earth. We are only here for a fleeting moment, so we have to push hard
and fight strong to get to where God ultimately wants us so that our ef-
forts ripple throughout the generations to come. You might be the first
in the line, just like Rahab. Or you may have a lineage going back as far
as you can see that all loved the Lord. Either way, there is something here
and now that God has for you to do that will reverberate down through
the generations. We have to get into that vault and pull out the promises
we can pass down. We have to storm the lair of our enemy and get back
the spoils lost and stolen from the generations before us. We need to
reclaim the wells the enemy has tried to stop up. We have to have His
Word in our hearts and on our lips. We need to know His voice and go
the way He leads. We have to love the way He loves. We have to live a life
that reflects who we truly are - daughters of the one true King. For me,
this is so worth the battle if one day my great-great-grandchild, the one I
will never meet on earth, comes to know Jesus because I was purposeful
to spend time with the King and lived a life shining with the legacy of Jesus Christ. I want my life to be such a reflection of Him that I can say to
my children, "This was my Dad's, and I want you to have it" and hand to
them their inheritance of salvation and promises and blessings from the
Kingdom vault. And I want it to impact them in such a powerful, life-al-

tering way that when it becomes their turn to pass on the inheritance to *their* children, they will be able to say, "This was my mother's, I want you to have it," and what they are handing off is Jesus.

THOUGHTS

THOUGHTS

Ten

MOTHER & NATIONS

ONE OF THE MOST AMAZING PRIVILEGES I have been given and blessed to walk in is when I get to be "mom" to children I did not birth. My husband and I were in youth ministry for almost eighteen years. During that ministry, we were able to love on kids, speak into their lives and give them direction and hope by pointing them to Jesus. We have had the honor of having them in our home and on vacations. Really any way they allowed us to have their lives woven in with ours, we wanted it. As adults, we have had many come back to us and thank us for loving them through what many deem the tough adolescent years, for being a safe place and letting them be real. We've been part of their weddings, asked to pray a blessing over their new babies, and invited to visit them in their new home towns where they now work and live. Some are in ministry, some are small business owners, and some work next to the President of the United States. All of them are so precious to us. I am always so thankful and humbled for all the youth God has entrusted to us.

When my boys joined the military, that blessing continued. In the military, you will find a powerful force of family surrounding your children. When they get through their training and God sets them where they will be stationed, that group of fellow servicemen and women in that place become a family to them. For some, like my boys, it's a second family. I cannot tell you what a blessing it was knowing that while my son was stationed in Japan, or deployed overseas not able to be home for Thanksgiving, or Christmas, or birthdays, that he had a family with him there, wherever he was, to surround him and be there for him when we couldn't.

Sadly, for others, you will find this new military family is the first and only family they have ever known. They do not have a mom and a dad and siblings and grandparents rooting them on, supporting them, and praying them through from home. In the cases of my boys, they had both of these scenarios in their military families. The beauty and blessing Mike and I have been given is that we were allowed into these military families as mom and dad. I consider all of them to be sons from other moms or brothers from other mothers to my boys. We have been given a blessing we never even thought to ask for, being the honorary parents of the nation's best.

Right after his graduation from Great Lakes Naval Training, Adam was assigned to Strike Fighter Squadron VFA-195, also known as the Dambusters. He was to go wherever those fighter jets went, and for four, long, crazy years, that place was Japan. During that time, however, God blessed our socks off by giving us the means and provision to travel there. A miracle God story for sure on how He brought that to pass, but even bigger was that He didn't just do it once, but between my husband, youngest son, and myself, we were able to make four trips! He is forever faithful.

Japan is a place I never had on my bucket list to visit, but wow, what an amazing place and experience. We were able to ride the bullet train from Tokyo to Hiroshima and Miyajima Island and visit Kyoto and Nagasaki. We even made it to Nagano, home of the 1998 winter Olympics, and also where the snow monkeys live. God was gracious in allowing us to have opportunities that many will never have. It was during these trips to Japan that we got to meet Adam's Navy "family." The guys in his line shack, the other sailors in his squadron, his CO's, pretty much everyone who spun in his new world in Japan.

On one of the visits, the Navy offered a Tiger Cruise, allowing family members to live a life at sea with their sailors on the aircraft carrier. Six months out of every year, Adam and his squadron would be deployed out on an aircraft carrier. During one of their returns from sea, they did what is called repositioning. The USS George Washington came into port in Nagasaki, and then family members, or Tigers as we were called, were able to board that ship and be part of an active aircraft carrier for the five days it took to reposition the ship from Nagasaki to Yokosuka where it was docked while not at sea. What an experience! To see the impeccable precision of the United States Navy and its flight deck in action was absolutely amazing. The berthing and daily life on the ship were also something that will always stick with me. I was forever changed.

The USS George Washington had a social media page that would post photos of the ports they would visit, incredibly impressive photos of the entire fleet as they sailed in formation, the flight deck in action, and all sorts of other events at sea. I loved seeing their posts. But the posts that would get me the most were the photos of them as they pulled back into the home port of Yokoskua after their time at sea. Sailors dressed in their dress whites encircled the ship's top decks as it came creeping into port, and family members lined the pier with homemade signs and waving flags welcoming their sailors home. I always had a pain in my heart and a catch in my throat every time my son would come "home" to Japan. I would imagine him looking out at the sea of signs and flags and smiling faces with happy tears coming down their cheeks as they ran and embraced their loved ones coming off that ship, and him realizing there was no one standing out there for him. This was much harder on me as a mom than it was for Adam, and I suppose if you were to ask him what the hardest part was of being stationed overseas, this probably would not even come up on his list, but it was definitely on mine. This time though, during the Tiger Cruise, while being honored guests aboard this ship, we got to be there for the homecoming! This time we were able to be there in person as this carrier came into port. We were able to stand on the top deck with sailors lining it in their dress whites. We were able to see the pier lined with signs and flags and the ever joyful reunion of families as they debarked the vessel. This time, our sailor wasn't coming home alone.

After coming off the Tiger Cruise, Mike and I were brought to the Atsugi Naval base with Adam and all the other sailors from the Dambuster Squadron. Atsugi was the base they called home. There was a bit of a walk from where we were dropped off at the main gate to where the single barracks were housed on base. We walked along with the sailors celebrating with them that they were finally off the ship, but what I witnessed next filled this mama's heart to the brim. As we rounded the final corner, I could see a large tent had been set up, and decorations were twirling about in the air. Women dressed in green Dambuster shirts had lined the street to the barracks, and they were clapping and cheering as we approached. These were the officer's wives from the Dambuster Squadron. They were there to welcome our sons and daughters home from six months at sea. In the tent, they were handing out homemade food, cake, and even laundry detergent. I watched with overwhelming gratitude at these "moms" and "sisters" loving on my son and being a family to all of those whose families could not be there to welcome them home. I was so undone; I had to walk away to keep from embarrassing my son with the blubbering mess I had become. As we walked through the gauntlet of officers' wives and their children, I saw something that was never posted on that social media page. I saw those who were there for Adam. Wives who, instead of being home welcoming their own husbands back from sea, were there to welcome my son.

When I had pulled myself together, I managed to make it over to the wife of the squadron commander, the one heading up this welcome party. I had had the privilege of meeting her husband on the aircraft carrier, and it didn't take long to realize he was an amazing man of faith. I thanked her for loving my son and for being the "welcome home" all the times we couldn't be.

If you haven't yet found it, you will soon discover there is something powerful about being a woman in the military family. A wife or mother of the one serving takes saying "support our troops" to the next level. When we couple that passion with the power of prayer and the love of Jesus Christ, we can change the atmosphere of the military. The military wives welcoming home the sailors there that day were doing just that. They were bringing the love of Jesus to all the single sailors. The commander's wife was being a mother to the nations and a mother to my son. I have no idea how far her love has reached, but I know it reached to me and to all those sailors coming through that welcome home tent that day. I know it reached to my son. This is the position we, you and I, and all the women like the commander's wife, have been called to. Together we are many, and together we can reach so very far.

Adam had the same roommate all four years in Japan. That roommate, along with several other young men from his squadron, has formed friendships, or should I say "familyships," that have lasted far beyond the confines of the military. We have hilarious, fun, touching, forever memories with these young men that have allowed us into their lives.

Our youngest son Matthew has been stationed stateside during his time in the Army, so we have been blessed to be able to spend more time with him and his Army family than that with Adam's Navy family. Some of them have called me Mama Motcheck from the moment they met me. Such a high honor to hold that title and one I am humbled and blessed to have. These army brothers have helped my son through really tough times, training, and deployments, which I will never understand or relate to, having never been there. Matthew has lost brothers from veteran suicide and from war. Only someone who has been through that can say, "I understand what you are going through." I will never be able to say those words to Matthew. I praise God that he has had these relationships and brothers to support him through it.

These young men (and also some young women) have become part of our extended family. There are many of them, too many to name, and quite frankly, some I only know by the nicknames or last names they are known by in the military, like Johnson, who would sharply remind all the other sailors to mind their tongues in my presence. Some have opened their hearts, shared life stories and experiences, future dreams, and past hurt. They have truly valued our presence in their lives.

These sons from other moms, each in their own capacity and way, have woven themselves into our lives. They have been in our home. They have been there for celebrations. They have been there and supported us for funerals. We've flown them in for moments we wanted to share with them. The beauty of it all is that they choose to love us back. Love does that. When you send it out, it comes back to you. They are part of our family. They know they are forever our boys.

My point in all of this is to awaken you to realize that you are not just the mother of your child serving. You have been called to be a mother of this nation. The call of "mother" isn't limited to those you have raised or birthed. It is a call to be a mother to the motherless.

Father to the fatherless, a defender of widows, is God in his holy dwelling.

PSALM 68:5

If from His holy dwelling God is a Father to those who do not have one, I believe He will also be the Mother to the motherless. YOU are His vessel for that very thing. Through you, He can bring His sons and daughters into a relationship with Him as you represent that part of His heart to them.

There are many scriptures in the Bible that reference God as having the traits of a mother. Those very traits are the ones He has breathed into you the moment He filled your lungs with His Yahweh breath. He has given you a piece of Himself for you to give out to others. To love the way He loves.

As a mother comforts her child, so will I comfort you.

ISAIAH 66:13

This passage references how God longs for a mother's comfort to actually be a mirror of His comfort. You are anointed to bring comfort, and not just any comfort, His comfort. Your heart is imprinted with His to comfort the way He comforts! All you have to do is offer what you already have. Holy Spirit in you will do the rest.

While Adam was deployed on the carrier or Matthew was deployed overseas, one of my favorite things to do was to let everyone around them know that their Mama Motcheck was thinking of them and praying them through. Big packages sent with love for all of them. Santa hats and stockings for all of them. Halloween costumes and candy in October for all of them. Bunny ears and peanut butter eggs on Easter for all of them. There were many that would receive nothing if not for those packages, and keeping morale up without encouragement from home is sometimes a really tough feat. I would ask Adam and Matthew to let me know if anyone around them needed anything in particular or needed extra love from a care package, and then Mike and I would fill that specific need.

When visiting, we would invite everyone, all of them, to dinner to celebrate them and to let them know how much they are all appreciated, being thought about, and being supported. It's how we love. It's the beat of our hearts as military parents. We care for the "orphans and widows"- James 1:27. We translate that to mean anyone and everyone who has no one is going to have us!

Sometimes out of the blue, my boys would send me only a name and an address. "Mom, send this guy some love." I never asked any questions; I just ran to the starting line. This race, I can win. My boys know one of my greatest joys is being a mother to those who may need one. My boys reaching out to me on behalf of someone who has no one shows they know how important having that love and support is. My sons long for their brothers from other mothers to have the support from "mom."

Look beyond your child to find opportunities to love as a mother loves. Like God has imprinted you to love. You have love enough to spread around, and there are those waiting for you, even if they just don't know it yet.

Once you start to look for open doors, you may be surprised at how God lets you shine His light into the places the enemy means to leave dark. When He gets you to that open door, WALK IN. Go in with boldness. You have a say over the open doors in the hearts He gives you. Having a say means you have the authority, anointing, and ability to impact the outcome of someone's life.

I was given such an opportunity with one of these boys. He found himself in a tough place. He had made a bad decision, which had the potential to change the course of his life. I had spent enough time with him that he had felt I was a safe enough place to pour out his heart to me more than once. From the time he was young straight up to this particular event, he had been through it. Now he stood at a place that could alter his life for the worse. He told me that he had to go up before a review board and that they would determine the outcome/result/punishment/resolution for this poor choice he made. The military doesn't put up with shenanigans, and

"

Look beyond your
child to find
opportunities to love
as a mother loves.
Like God has
imprinted you to love.

————

from the outside looking in, this didn't look like it was going to be in his favor. But God! I knew this was a door that God was opening. I took the chance and did what I would have done with my own sons. I spoke into his life. I told him that he is not his past. He is not his bad choice. He is not his mistake. This event will not define him for the rest of his life. I told him that I believed in who he was and who he was called to be. I told him that God is a God of second chances, and He can be that God of second chances for him too. I told him that I would be praying for him and that God would see him through this. It wasn't over. I was on his team. God was on his team. I was expecting God to move.

Then I had to leave and go home. We did not know when the review would be because...well... military, but he was going to keep me posted and let me know. Every time he came to mind, I would pray. A few weeks later I got a text that the review was happening. I thanked him for letting me know. I told him I was going immediately to talk to God on the matter and that I was praying him through all the way and not to worry.

After this discussion with him, I had to head to an appointment a half-hour drive away. During that drive, I did what any mom does for her son when he is facing a giant that looks bigger than he does. I started warring for that boy. I was in my battle gear, sword and shield in hand, and I was not getting off that wall until God finished it. I said, "God, you can do this. You are a God of second chances, and if you want to show him that, today would be the day to do it. Let him know that everything I have proclaimed and declared about you is true! Let him see your love is greater than his past, that you cover his wrongs, and you give footing to those who slip. God, move in that room. Bring your favor and light. Let them see he is worth more than what they see as a write-up on a paper. God, this is not a mountain to you, and you can move it. Let hope arise, and his enemies be scattered. There may be a giant in the land, but when he runs at it with the Name of the Lord God Almighty, it cannot stand." I was crying. I was yelling. I was beating my steering wheel. I was singing worship at the top of my lungs. I was declaring. I meant business. This was a son that God had entrusted to me to intercede for. I wasn't messing around. I did this the entire thirty-minute drive. If there was ever a fervent prayer, this was it. The lioness God refers to so many times in the Bible arose within me. This was my cub, and satan, you best be backing up! By the time I had reached the parking lot where my meeting was taking place, I felt a release that was almost a physical lifting. I cannot explain it, but I knew that I knew that I knew that God was going to see this through. Something had broken. Something was won. Just what, I didn't yet know.

Then the waiting. Waiting. Waiting for him to let me know how it had come out. Then the text I had been waiting for finally came through; The review board had dismissed it. They were giving him a second chance.

Yeah, they are! Thank you, Jesus!! Tears and shouts, and claps and dancing of praise ensued next. We serve an awesome God. He's a God of second chances, and He wanted this young man to know it.

A month or so after receiving that news, I headed down for another visit with my son. As I stood outside the airport watching for his car, I was surprised to find my son hadn't come alone. In the driver's seat was the young man who I had prayed for. I was honored that he, too, had made the trip to get me. After a few moments, it became clear that part of why he had come was because he had something on his heart. He gave me a hug and said, "Mama Motcheck, I am thoroughly convinced it is because of your prayers that I was given a second chance." I was wrecked to hear those words. I was over the moon thankful that God had given me an open door, but even more grateful that I was allowed into this young man's heart. His circumstances led him to a vulnerable place where I was able to point him to a God that loves him more than anyone on this earth ever could. God's movement in his life became real in that moment. It was demonstrating the Mother heart of God to him that then gave me room to speak into his life. I am now given room to help him navigate. I am able to say, "Now live right and make wise choices!" and that will have merit because he knows he is loved by me and by God.

We have a say. We can change the course of the lives of children we did not bear because we have a gifting and a calling that cannot be revoked— the call to be a mom. God will bring into your life those who need to know what being loved by a godly mother feels like. Some just need a God wink in their lives to be reminded who they are and Whose they are. Like this young man. Then there are some that literally have no home. It is heart-breaking to find that there are some who never receive a care package or letter from home. No one comes to their graduations or pinning ceremonies. No one back home is praying for their safe return. There is nothing to hang onto while in the throngs of everything the military brings and throws at them. No going home for the holidays. No sense of belonging. Being made privy to that saddening truth makes something rise up in me to say, "You will never know the feeling of being alone, forgotten, or unwanted again. Not on my watch!" I'm able to open my arms wide and give them a home.

The beauty of the gospel and love of Jesus that we carry in us is that it gives us the privilege to enter into areas that people who don't carry it will never get to enter. When the Spirit of God is on the move, He will open doors that no man can shut (Revelations 3:7). Even if they don't walk with Jesus themselves, the unsaved will pull towards you because they know you do! When God formed us in our mother's wombs, it set into motion a desire inside all of us to find Him. We not only carry His breath, but we carry a spirit within us that longs, aches, and searches to be with Him. Those who have never known Him don't know exactly what they are searching for. They chase after things to fill the longing by trying to find answers to the big questions of life. Why are we here? What is my purpose? Is there really a God? When we are given the open door to bring His presence into their life, just like the tide cannot help but be pulled by the moon, the spirit within them cannot help but be pulled to that which we carry - Him. Even if they don't know Him, something rises within them to believe that just maybe our faith is big enough to reach Him for their sake as well.

This is something that has been demonstrated since Bible days. We read over and over how people following or worshiping pagan gods knew the only one who could do something was the One true God. They would ask those who walked with the Lord to call on their God to move on their behalf. In the book of Jonah, we see the sailors yell this at Jonah when the boat they are in comes into a bad storm. They were out of their own ideas and means to save themselves and the ship, but they also knew there was a God who could help them. It just wasn't their god. It was Jonah's God. So they yell at Jonah, who is asleep at the bottom of the ship:

Now Jonah doesn't "call" on the Lord because Jonah is currently in trouble with God for not obeying, and he knows the Lord isn't going to aid him in his running away. What he *does* tell them is that he worships the Lord, the God of Heaven, who made the sea and land. He also tells them that unless they throw him overboard, the storm will not stop. Jonah testifies to the sailors about the goodness of God and that he worships Him even when he is in total disobedience! Come on! What a great testimony.

Maybe the most amazing part of this story isn't even about the whale, while that's super cool and all. The most amazing part to me is the fact that these sailors get to see the hand of God in action, and because of this, they find salvation in the one true God (see vs. 1:16).

This is still happening today. Being a mother to the nations may lead you to children who believe God couldn't possibly hear them should they call out to Him. They don't see themselves as sons and daughters of the one true King. They can't imagine any reason why His ear would be inclined to them. They may not see Him as a good Father who always has their good in mind. A Father with plans to prosper them and bring them blessings and an abundant life. They believe the lies from the pit of hell that they will never be worthy of God's love, let alone His blessings. They believe their sin is too great and their past too awful to ever get near a loving God and have Him move in their lives. However, most of them believe if someone else asks on their behalf, that person just may get God to move *for* them. I see it like siblings arguing about which one will go ask dad for permission. They choose which child will go talk to dad by deciding which one they believe has the most favor with the father, or has the most guts, thus, the best chance of getting the yes answer they are looking for.

The military sons and daughters God leads you to love may not believe they have any favor with God and that they can do nothing to persuade Him to listen or care, but they also know He is more than able to change the course or the circumstance if only they could get someone else to go talk to Him. This way of thinking will bring them to lean on you to get God to move for them. What a privilege! I have never had one of those who God has led me to love say, "Please don't pray for me," even if they proclaim to not believe in God at all. I believe there will always be that part of them that is wanting to connect with their Creator and realize that they have nothing to lose if He doesn't exist, but everything to gain if He does. What an honor it is when they grant me permission to go into the Throne room on their behalf. Oh, sweet child... You betcha I'll go ask Dad! The greatest thing I will ever get to do is to show them, He's not only moving when I talk to Him, but He's longing to move when THEY talk to Him. For all the times they felt they didn't fit or belong and could not gain access, I get to take them in to meet the King! Not only meet Him but let them find that there has always been a seat at His table for them. Seeing your name card placed at a seat at the table you have never felt valued or loved enough to sit at- Wow! I still remember when I saw my name card there and how I still have no words for that God encounter.

That is what I want for all of those of whom God grants me an audience.

We get the honor and privilege of stepping in. We will become that home. The safe place. The constant. You are the mother of this nation. Even more, by using your gift and calling to love those with that love of a mother that God has breathed into you, you also become the mother of many nations. The ones you love on, take those promises of God that you have deposited into them wherever the military sends them. Wherever their boots touchdown, wherever deployments and military operations take them. Those you wrap up with prayer, those you point to Jesus, those whose lives you alter by walking into the ordained steps God has lined up for *you*, and helping them find *theirs*, that anointing and spiritual covering goes with them. Your prayers then reach outside of our national borders, and you become the mother of nations.

Ask me, and I will make the nations your inheritance, the ends of the earth our possession.

PSALM: 2:8

Therefore go and make disciples of all nations.

MATTHEW 28:19

. . . and you will be my witnesses in Jerusalem, and in all of Judea, and Samaria, and to the ends of the earth.

ACTS 1:8

God has offered us nations as our inheritance and the ends of the earth as someplace attainable if only we ask and then walk it out. How do we touch nations while remaining in the place we stand? How do we get to the ends of the earth with the gospel of Jesus Christ? A couple of ways. First, by being mission-minded and giving of our time, talents, and treasures to those who are going to all the places we will never get to go. My husband and I have faithfully given financially to missionaries who are going to the nations my feet will never set foot in. God had one Son, and one of the things He was to demonstrate here on earth was the heart of missions. You will see that in the two New Testament scriptures, Matthew 28:19 and Acts 1:8 are both red letters verses in the Bible. That means they were words spoken by Jesus. If we want to be like Jesus, we have to have a mindset that includes getting the gospel out globally. So, my husband and I support those who are going to do just that, taking their families and going to places that have never heard of Jesus Christ. The second way is by us sharing the love of Jesus Christ, by getting the gospel proclaimed to as many people who will listen because who knows how far their reach will be?

The military kids Mike and I have poured into have taken the gospel within them to some far-off places. Australia, Thailand, Philippines, Korea, Hong Kong, Afghanistan, Syria, Guam, Singapore, all throughout the United States, any place they have ever vacationed, their hometowns, and the homes of their families and friends. Whether they realize it or not, every place they have set their feet, God has gone too.

Now, I'm not sure which nations are mine, but whichever ones God has set aside for my inheritance, I will spend my life here on earth making sure they know His Name. Every one of the military kids I share the gospel with, everyone I have loved the way God has imprinted my mother's heart to love, is part of my nations. Where that gospel and love spread has the potential to get to more of my nations and also to theirs. Wherever they go, I am believing they will leave a deposit of God behind. Won't it be something for us to one day get to Heaven and have God show us just how far our impact for the Kingdom has reached?

Your military sons and daughters are taking with them the deposits of God literally to the ends of the earth. Your impact and reach may seem limited, but when you send all of these sons and daughters off with God, His reach knows no bounds. Start using that gift of God that knows no end. Your gift, calling, and anointing of mom. Deposit in them the gifts of eternity. As we pour into them, it starts a drip, and that one drip will start a ripple effect that goes farther than we will ever know until we get to Heaven. It might seem like such a small thing, but God is the God of small beginnings. We just have to start the work and then watch and see how far He takes it!

THOUGHTS

eleven

HILLS & MOUNTAINS

THE WORD MOUNTAIN is used close to 500 times in the Bible. We find it used in reference to an actual mountain or location on the map, such as the Mount of Olives, Mount Caramel, and Mount Sinai. When referencing the longest message Jesus delivered in our Bible text, we recognize it by the location, The Sermon on the Mount. There is also the Mount of Transfiguration, where Jesus stands face to face with Moses and Elijah. Some pretty big biblical events happen on the mountains. The one that is most precious to me is the mountain called Calvary. The hill Jesus died on. Before I ever knew Him, He loved me and gave up His life for me. He paid the price of my guilt and bought me back from the grips of sin so that I am able to live a life walking in His victory and abundant love.

Mountains are the ultimate symbol of stability and long-standing. They can be known as the pinnacle of achievement and victory once the summit has been reached. The spiritual mountains we climb and the summits we reach gets us closer to God's truth. We gain the high ground so we can win the battle. Then there are those mountains on which the enemy stands in our way, and no matter how hard we try, it seems we cannot reach the summit and gain the victory.

Mountains don't move. Or do they? The awesome thing about going through life as a daughter of the King is that He controls my mountains. One of the declarations I often pray out is, "this is not a mountain to God." He is the one that has ordained the path I am meant to walk on. This means that the mountains I am meant to conquer, I will, and the mountains that are meant to be moved, He will.

Mountains bring about a feeling of impossibility. They can make us feel small and insignificant, knowing we do not have the human ability or strength to take it on. I believe that is why God filled our Bible with so many passages about mountains not behaving like mountains when we come at them with faith so that we can see that nothing is impossible.

Jesus replied, "Because you have so little faith, I tell you the truth, if you have faith as small as a mustard seed, you can say to this mountain, 'Move from here to there,' and it will move. Nothing will be impossible for you."

MATTHEW 17:20

"Truly I tell you, if anyone says to his mountain 'Go throw yourself into the sea,' and does not doubt in their heart but believes that what they say will happen, it will be done for them."

MARK 11:23

In these verses, Jesus is telling us in His red letters that the impossible becomes possible when we have faith! When Jesus says "truly," that's a truth I want to be seeded deep in my heart. The truth that with Him and the victory bought on Calvary, we can move mountains. Believing that your faith can move mountains might be the first mountain you'll need to climb.

Faith is being sure of what we hope for and certain of what we do not see.

HEBREWS 11:1

I needed to climb this mountain too. Whatever I was hoping for, I needed to be sure of that. I needed to do it for me and for my children. When I prayed, I needed to have an unshakeable faith that I believed that God was big enough to do what I was saying He could. What *His Word* says He could. So, like I did with the rock in the chapter Rocks and Lilies, I wanted to find a seed I could look at as I took on this mountain of faith. The scripture says that if I have faith as small as a mustard seed, I can command mountains to pick themselves up and throw themselves into the sea. That's pretty amazing. I wanted that! But, what if I went bigger. I decided I didn't just want mustard seed size faith. I wanted bigger. I set out about my home to find the biggest seed I could, and I settled on the avocado. If mustard seed size faith can move a mountain, how much more could avocado seed size faith do? I took that seed and set it on the window ledge above my kitchen sink. It still sits there today, so I have a daily reminder of just how possible the impossible becomes when I move with God. This is a truth I want to pass to my children.

The number one thing I want for my children is to know Jesus Christ as their personal Lord and Savior. Above all things, no matter what I am feeling or desiring or seeing with human eyes, that will always be my number one want for their lives. I want them to know the truth of the Gospel of Jesus Christ.

I have no greater joy than to hear that my children are walking in the truth.

3 JOHN 1:4

There needs to be a foundation laid before anything can ever be built. The foundation I need to lay for my children to have a life walking in truth requires blocks from the Kingdom. Nothing will stand, nothing will have the ability to remain, and nothing will be stable until we first establish the foundation we are going to be building on.

Consequently, you are no longer foreigners and aliens, but fellow citizens with God's people and members of God's household, built on the foundation of the apostles and prophets, with Christ Jesus himself as the chief cornerstone. In him, the whole building is joined together and rises to become a holy temple in the Lord. And in him, you too are being built together to become a dwelling in which God lives by his Spirit.

EPHESIANS 2:19-22

Jesus Christ is the cornerstone of that foundation. If we start with Jesus as our cornerstone, our lives become a dwelling place where God lives by his Spirit! That's what I want! For me and my household to have lives built on Jesus Christ. That requires that every block we place upon the foundation that Jesus started as the anchored cornerstone *must* be something Jesus can hold. It must be something that can be built upon His truth, Kingdom truth, or it will simply tumble off the wall. He will never hold anything that doesn't represent or reflect the Father. If we are to win any form of battle with and for our children, we must erect a structure that cannot be shaken. The walls built on the cornerstone of Jesus Christ never waver, the blocks never come apart, and those walls can never be breached. The dwelling built with blocks of Kingdom truth with Jesus himself holding it all together will forever stand. That is where we must dwell and run back to when the battles are over.

In our home, when we spoke about these blocks of truth with our boys, we called them "hills we would die on." This is a twist on the military act of taking and capturing the hill or the high ground and then defending it even unto death. Maybe you have heard it used in the negative form "this is not a hill I'm willing to die on." The hills I am willing to die on are the hills I know Jesus is standing and defending alongside me. On those hills there are stones of truth and victory that can be placed upon the wall He is holding together. The hills I am not willing to die on are the ones I find I am standing on alone. On those hills, I will only find stones for the rubble pile.

"This We'll Defend" is the motto emblazoned on the United States Army flag. Being military mamas and spirit-filled shield maidens, it seems only fitting that we should define those hills worth dying for, sorting out those worth defending from those that should never be a hill in our lives to begin with. If nothing else has driven you to claim your spiritual ground and territory at this point, being thrust into the military life will. It has a way of stripping away the nonsense and bringing into focus what needs to remain.

"Once more, I will shake not only the earth but also the heavens." The words "once more" indicate the removing of what can be shaken that is, created things so that what cannot be shaken may remain.

HEBREWS 12:26-27

We need to start by deciding what hills of truth we want to fight for and then defend. Different from the standards of behavior we identified in the chapter Motchecks and Standards, these are truths that we choose to believe and live by, no matter what we see or feel. However, in the same fashion as the standards, we also pull these truths straight from scripture. If God said it, He means it. Every letter in our Bible is God-breathed, and as we read God's written Word, it's as if He is speaking and reading those very words aloud to only us in that moment. He will show us things in scripture every time we go into it. He will reveal truths and promises. The more Kingdom hills you claim, the more territory you will possess. God will give us clear direction of that which is worth fighting for, conquering, and then defending. When our whole world feels like it is being shaken, and we are under attack, we are held tight in our dwelling place that cannot be shaken. Everything that does not point to the Kingdom or His promises, anything that Jesus Himself cannot hold in His hands, is shakable and will fall over into a pile of rubble so that all that *is* of Him, the unshakable things can remain.

We don't have time for shakable things, ladies. We need to stop trying to hang onto those things that will never remain. We are in a battle, and there is never any neutral ground. It's either going to be the land you possess and hold or land you allow the enemy to remain in, or worse, take from you. The enemy never gives up on trying to take from you the promises of God. He's crafty and methodical. He can be stealthy and patient, waiting for you to show any sign of weakness. His plan is to hold you back from advancing while simultaneously trying to snatch the ground you already have. One of his best tricks is to use our feelings and emotions and our everyday lives to distract us from the big picture. It's actually a great tactic. I have many times lost sight of the big picture while I was distracted by something the enemy keeps highlighting. Not only have I been distracted, but I have found myself sitting in the pile of rubble which has zero defenses from the enemy's blows. Fear starts to take hold. Fear paralyzes us as warriors, and it paralyzes us as mothers. When I find that I am parenting or warring from fear, I have to remember that Jesus cannot hold fear, so this is not a hill He will defend or a mountain He will help me climb. The best things that God has for us live on the other side of fear. We need to push past fear to find the victory!

There is a small story in scripture that many times just gets skimmed over. It's found in 2 Samuel 23:9-10 and also in 1 Chronicles 11:12-14. It's truly one of my favorite stories. This is one of the stories about David's Mighty Men and a seemingly silly battle over a field full of barley, or in some translations, it's a field of lentils. Either way, be it barley or lentils, it doesn't matter. It wasn't a battle over the crop; it was a battle for God's promise. You see, that very plot of land was part of the land God promised to Israel. The enemy, the Philistine army, didn't care what was on the land but only that they had to take it from David and push Israel's territorial lines back. You will see in this story that the troops, the bulk of David's army, ran from this battle and from the Philistines who were advancing towards them. Many of David's soldiers didn't believe or feel that this field was worth dying over. They were moved or led by fear. What they were seeing with their eyes was, after all, just lentils or barley. Big whoop, right? Sadly, they missed what the battle was really about. It wasn't about the barley; it was about protecting God's promise. This was bigger than what they could see or feel.

Defending something you might not see or feel in the natural, but know in your spirit to be worth dying for, takes faith. It takes guts. It takes a shield maiden warrior. If you keep reading the text, you will see that the importance of this battle did not get missed by The Mighty Men, the men who were running after God. When they looked at that field, they didn't see it as a measly crop that may or may not be of any earthly value. They saw it as a bigger picture of territory that God Himself handed to Israel. The value of this land was beyond earthly comprehension. If God gave that field to them, it was ultimately for Kingdom purposes. Anything that has Kingdom purpose is worth fighting for, even if you don't see or feel it yet. The Mighty Men took their stand in the middle of that field and defended that which was promised by God even if it meant their own death. A hill, or in this case a field, they were willing to die on. The scriptures tell us that Eleazar took this battle seriously enough that he fought and defended that God-promised field until his hand was frozen to his sword. God's favor was on him, and with him, and because he warred for that which was

God's, God brought the victory. Whenever you fight for the promises God has given you, He fights alongside you.

Don't let the enemy tell you God's promises aren't worth fighting for. If you don't continue to stand and claim those promises, the enemy will be sure to try and take them out from under you. Don't come off of your hills! Remaining on top of them is not always easy, but then war never is. You may find yourself in the most fierce and bloodied game of king-on-the-mountain with the enemy that you've ever been in, but don't you dare give up. The enemy will surely try to force your feet to slip off your hill of peace when your son or daughter is deployed to a war zone. Sometimes staking a claim on the hill of joy seems impossible when the enemy keeps lobbing rubble of PTSD at your child. Perhaps your child's health or injury is driving you to climb, conquer and defend the hill of "by His stripes, we are healed," and while fighting for that hill, you see the enemy coming out from the bushes to attack your hill of hope.

It's a lot of work to keep gaining ground while maintaining your territory at the same time because the enemy will never stop coming at you or your children. But I have some great news! We serve a God who never sleeps and never slumbers, and He's a God who never fails. This battle belongs to the Lord. He will block every one of the enemy's blows if we remain in His dwelling place, keeping our eyes on Him and not on what we can see or feel in the natural.

On one of our trips to Japan visiting Adam, we had the incredible opportunity to hike Mount Fuji. Our plan was to hike halfway up, stay in the offered lodging there on the mountain, and then hike the remaining portion of the mountain very early the next morning in time to see the sunrise from the summit. It was going to be epic! Who gets that opportunity? We were super excited. The first part of the plan went off without a hitch. It was a beautiful sunny day, and the hike was gorgeous. We reached the station as planned, had some dinner, and then went to sleep in the lodge, which was actually an innumerable number of sleeping bags laid touching side by side in one big open room. This was an experience in itself; sleeping shoulder to shoulder with strangers. Very early the next morning, one of the staff at the lodge came up into that big room, which was now pretty full of people with the same plan we had, and told us the weather had forced them to close the mountain pass to the summit until daylight. There was an audible sigh in that room because this meant that none of us would reach the summit by sunrise due to weather. That didn't sound great, and when daylight broke, we could see why they had closed it. It was pouring rain. I mean, it was coming down in sheets, and the winds were so high that it drove the rain in a horizontal direction straight into our faces. And if that wasn't bad enough, the fog was so thick you couldn't see much farther than an arm's reach in front of you. Standing outside the lodge, we had to decide if we were going to keep going up or cut our hike short and start heading down. Either way, it was going to be cold, wet, and miserable. There was a little store at the station where we had stayed, and it happened to sell some rain gear. We bought what we could, but to get the complete visual, you have to remember that nothing they sell in Japan is made to fit American bodies. Seeing my over six-foot-tall son squeezed into what looked like on him to be a blue toddler size rain suit would have been far more hilarious if we weren't in such dire straits.

We decided we were going up to see this thing through, realizing that it would take us that much longer to get out of the weather. However, we hadn't come this far to quit now, and we had meant to see it through. As we began to climb in the wind and fog and horizontal rain with the air getting thinner with every step, Mike and I started to doubt we had made the right decision. Trying to stay sure-footed on the wet terrain was adding to the slow crawl to the top. When I say crawl, there are actually some really tough places where we had all four of our hands and feet, and sometimes even our knees making contact with the mountain at the same time. Adam, who was fit as a fiddle, had been trekking ahead of us during the entire hike the day before, and even with the conditions the second day had thrown us, he was always far ahead. We'd find him waiting for us from point to point, taking pictures and being more than patient with his two, forty-something parents who were irritatingly much, much slower.

On Mount Fuji, the ascent climb is on one side of the mountain, which has switchbacks making the incline a bit more manageable, and for the descent, there is another trail that is pretty steep and almost a straight line down to the bottom. There are certain places on the mountain where those two paths run close together, and you can skip off the ascending trail and start your descent on the other if you weren't fully committed to the climb. As we got nearer to the summit that second day, Adam recognized that his mama was struggling. I was wet, I was cold, I was tired, I had an altitude headache, and the air felt mighty thin. At that time in my life, I was also fighting through some health issues that caused me to be anemic, which magnified the lightheadedness from the altitude. This was just about as miserable as it could get. Switching over to the descending trail was looking better with every step I took. At one point, when we met up with Adam, I was standing against a railing and contemplating quitting the climb. Getting myself back to thicker air and warm, dry clothes sounded far better than reaching the summit of that blasted mountain that clearly didn't want us on it to begin with. Adam, however, wasn't about to let me quit. He knew if I quit, I would forever regret it. I had come so far and fought through some of the toughest elements, and I was far closer to the top than I realized. The rain and fog blocked my vision, so I had no idea where we were on that mountain. He knew, though, as this was not his first climb on Mt Fuji, just how close I was to the summit. Then my son did the only thing he knew to do to get me up to finish that climb. He led me up the mountain. He slowed his pace to match that of what he knew I could keep up with, staying just one step at a time ahead of me. All he told me to do was focus on where he was placing his foot, and that's exactly what I did. I was able to keep my head down and my face out of the pelting rain. Without looking around, or up, or down, or worrying that my foot would slip, I followed the steps he was leading for me. One step and then the next. I wasn't thinking about the cold, or thin air, or anything I felt. I wasn't counting on what I could or couldn't see; I simply followed what I knew. I knew if I followed him and the trail he was blazing before me, if I just kept going by placing my foot in the very place his foot had just been, if I didn't quit, he would safely get me to the top. The mountain wasn't so steep, and it wasn't so hard to conquer when I remained focused on where my steps were being led.

Remember, mountains don't behave like mountains when God comes on the scene. He lays them flat.

---

*The mountains melt like wax before the Lord, before the
Lord of all the earth.*

PSALM 97:5

*The mountains melt beneath Him and the valleys split
apart, before the fire, like water rushing down a slope.*

MICAH 1:4

Ladies, there are going to be mountains that feel like my experience on
Mount Fuji. There will be a hill you are fighting to conquer and defend,
but getting to the top of it may be taking its toll on you. You may be climbing the mountain of sound mind that God has promised in 2 Timothy
1:7 over your soldier, but all you can see are the enemy's repeated blows of
depression. You may find this is one of the most miserable hikes of your
life. You may be looking around and seeing nothing but defeat. You may
feel like you are slipping on all the rocks and terrain and making no prog-
ress. Remember what truth lays at the top! The truth that His promise of
a sound mind over your life and your children's lives are worth fighting
for. Stand your ground. Find your grit. Fight until your hand is frozen
to the sword, but do not turn around and do not retreat down the other
side. Put your focus on Him. Follow the trail He is blazing before you,
and just like my son did for me, He will get you to the top. Mountains
are not mountains to God. If there is a mountain in your way, He will
move it. If there is a mountain He wants you to climb, you will possess
it. Even if you can't see the summit, keep going and trust His leadership.

The summit is there! Then, once you reach the summit, possess the land!

Once the children of Israel had finally reached the promised land after a weary journey of forty years fighting to get there, Caleb goes and claims what is rightfully his. The land promised by God.

I, however, followed the Lord my God wholeheartedly. So on that day Moses swore to me, 'The land on which your feet have walked will be your inheritance and that of your children forever, because you have followed the Lord my God wholeheartedly.'

JOSHUA 14:8B-9

Now, give me this mountain that the Lord promised me on that day.

JOSHUA 14:12

Caleb followed the Lord and then had grit enough to go claim and possess the mountain, the land that he was promised.

Search out the hills of God's promises and claim them for you and your children! Let them be hills you will die on. Fight for them until your hand is frozen to your sword. God will fight with you and for you to bring about a great victory!

THOUGHTS

THOUGHTS

Twelve

PRAYER & HEAVEN

His plane just landed in the states.

THAT'S THE TEXT I RECEIVED when my youngest son was finally stateside and home from his first deployment in Afghanistan. On hearing that sentence, the wind was completely squeezed from my lungs. Every last bit of the breath I had been holding for the previous nine months came out in a rush so great that I thought I might pass out. I had to sit down. I started to hyperventilate as my lungs tried to recover and reinflate themselves with air. My human flesh seemed unable to contain the spiritual victory I was standing in! For months I had prayers going up sometimes as loud battle cries, sometimes through chokes of tears and brokenness, sometimes through bold declarations, and sometimes with nothing but groans and sighs. It was all for this moment. He was safe. He was home. Thank you, Jesus!

If you think back, all while they are growing up, you may remember how your prayers have changed over time. Your prayers may have started before they were ever in your womb, asking God for a safe pregnancy, an easy birth, that they would sleep just one full night! Please, God! Then you find yourselves praying for the things wrapped in the next stage of their lives and then the next until you find yourself standing with me, praying for our military children. I've been talking and petitioning God their entire lives. Some of them were selfish prayers that I think God just smiles at and understands the heart and weariness of a mother. Then there are times when I sought God out fervently on behalf of my boys. Nights I didn't sleep. Days I fasted for a breakthrough. Tears staining the pages of my Bible. If anything pushes me to fight for Heaven to move, it would be my boys. What pushes me even further is my boys in the military.

How we pray is pivotal to the true outcomes we are seeking. I remember a time my son's high school football team made it to the semi-finals, something that was pretty much unheard of for the Shelby football team. This was a big deal. The whole town had been doing parade send-offs for the team's bus as they drove to the games. Fans showed up in droves to cheer them on. It was such an amazing time in our community. The state playoffs were played on random, neutral fields, so we had to drive hours away to where they would be playing. On the way to the stadium for one of the games, I was praying. The first prayer a mom wants to pray in this situation is, "God! Let the Shelby Tigers take this win! In Jesus' name, amen." I am that mom, and that was the prayer I was wanting to pray. I really wanted them to win! But as soon as this prayer was forming and about to come out of my lips, God showed me that there was a mom on the other team that was wanting to pray this very same prayer. It instantly gave me a different perspective on praying for this game. God already knew who was going to win this game. Both moms are praying the same thing, but only one mom would have the "win" as her answered prayer. The second mom would seemingly not have her prayer answered. Those prayers from those two moms put God in an impossible situation. He could not answer yes to both moms this time. Both teams cannot win. One team has to lose. He cannot partner with those types of prayers. It made me realize that if I wanted God to partner with my prayers, I had to change the way I pray. I had to pray prayers that did not put God in an impossible situation. The true outcome I was after wasn't that my son would win or lose the game, but that the reason God had placed my son in this moment would have its way in his life. When I asked God how to pray for this game, and what I found myself doing is praying scriptures over my son and his team, the coaches, the other team, and their coaches. These prayers He can partner with! Looking back, I believe this game had a far bigger purpose than just the Tigers making the playoffs. God used this time in my son's life to teach me how to pray His Word and victory over my son in a way He can partner with and answer. He was teaching me to pray *from* victory. Something that would become very important down the line when my sons joined the military.

The first thing military moms standing on the front lines have to remember is to always pray *from* the place of victory! We don't pray *for* it because we already have it. There are blanket prayers we tend to pray out and hope we move Heaven with them. "Keep my children safe" is an example of one of those prayers. While God will hear it, it doesn't engage your faith like when we start from the Cross and pray from there. The victory bought on the Cross means we have already won this battle; we just have to call it down and believe it is for us and for our children. Jesus opened Heaven for us so that we have access to the Creator of the universe, and He wants to move in your life. He wants to partner with your prayers. He wants you to pray out His Word and truth over your children with avocado seed size faith so all of Heaven can be put in motion and bring your answered prayers to fruition. We have to believe *what* we pray, and we have to pray in a way He can answer.

Faith is the currency of Heaven. Heaven moves when we believe our own prayers. This is a great time to get your imaginations activated. God gave us an imagination for a reason. If we can see it, it's easier to believe it. When we don't see it in the natural, we need to learn to see it in the spirit. Close your eyes and imagine His truth coming to pass. Do you have a child who needs physical healing? Imagine him or her whole and healed. The victory on the Cross is that we ARE healed by the stripes of Christ. Not *might* be healed. Not *may* be healed. The Bible says, "*are* healed." That's a prayer from victory and a prayer He can answer. Do you have a child far from the Lord? Imagine him or her behind a pulpit. Imagine your child reading the Bible and memorizing scripture. Pray into that. Don't pray wimpy prayers. "Lord, I hope one day he comes back to you" is a wimpy prayer. Instead, pray the bold prayer;

> God your Word says that whoever believes in you rivers of living water will flow from within them (John 7:38). Your Word says that our sons and daughters will come from afar (Isaiah 60:4) and that they will prophesy (Acts 2:17) and that they shall not perish but have everlasting life (John 3:16). I am calling my child back to right standing with you. You are a God of second chances and reconciliation (2 Corinthians 5:19), and you can redeem everything that seems to be lost. The Word sent out from Your mouth over

my child, and the blessings and promises established over his life will not return empty, and it will accomplish the purpose for which you sent it (Isaiah 55:11).

In Jesus' name, AMEN!

Now that is a prayer packed with promise and prophecy that God can partner with and launch Heaven out to fulfill. Pray from victory. Use your eyes of faith to see it come to pass.

Set your mind on things above and not on earthly things.

COLOSSIANS 3:2

We have not received the spirit of the world but the Spirit who is from God, that we may understand what God has freely given us. This is what we speak, not in words taught us by human wisdom, but in words taught by the Spirit, expressing spiritual truths in spiritual words.

1 CORINTHIANS 2:12-13

There are things He has freely given us that He wants us to understand. You aren't going to find these things being led by the world. They will be revealed, *taught* to us by the Spirit. God wants to honor and fulfill His Word over your life. That is who He is and what He does. He is always in a good mood, and He is always on your side. If He loves us enough to send His only Son to die on a cross to buy us back from the grip of satan's wrath, He will stop at nothing to get you out and keep you out of that grip. The work was already completed. As we pray out and call down those things that are alive and active in the heavenly realm, God can fulfill them in the natural realm because that is His divine nature. Pray out specifics. Spend time reading your Bible and pray out those things you find in scripture. We combat the enemy with the Word of God and having the faith to believe that it is true.

We are in a battle that is not against flesh and blood (Ephesians 6:12). If our battle is not against flesh and blood, then we can't rely on our own devices to win the war. Our greatest weapon is the Word of God. Against the Word, the enemy cannot stand.

As the Philistine moved closer to attack him, David ran quickly toward the battle line to meet him. Reaching into his bag and taking out a stone, he slung it and struck the Philistine on the forehead. The stone sank into his forehead, and he fell facedown on the ground. So David triumphed over the Philistine with a sling and a stone.

1 SAMUEL 17:48-50

At first glance, it would appear that it was David's artillery that trumped Goliath's infantry, but we need to back up a few verses to see what gave David the courage to run towards the battle.

David said to the Philistine, (Goliath) "You come against me with the sword and spear and javelin, but I come against you in the name of the Lord Almighty, the God of

the armies of Israel, whom you have defied. This day the
Lord will hand you over to me."

1 SAMUEL 17:45

David did not kill Goliath with a slingshot. He killed him with the Name of the Lord and his faith in knowing that nothing can stand against God. The giant he was looking down in the natural was no match for the weaponry of Heaven David carried within himself.

As you spend time in prayer over your sons and daughters, the Holy Spirit will reveal things for you to join with Heaven on. Sometimes the thing we believe to be a mother's intuition is actually the Holy Spirit revealing something to us regarding our children. Things that you could only know because God knows. God will show you what to pray for. One particular time before my son Matthew left on deployment I was led to call him and tell him to pay attention when he saw the color purple. It was a very distinct shade. I didn't know the full picture of why or what it would be, but I knew he had to pay attention when he saw it, so that is all I was able to tell him. Months later, I was sent a picture of him standing beside a medic that was deployed with him, and they were standing inside what looked like an upscale building in the Middle East. I couldn't stop looking at that photograph. Something (now I know it was the Holy Spirit) kept drawing me to it and compelled me to keep pushing forward to get more details about that building. I finally asked Matthew about that building in the photograph. He then pulled up another picture, and this one showed the outside of this same building. There it was! A bell rang in my spirit. The door to that building was the exact shade of purple that God had shown me months before, and standing right next to that door was my son dressed in full battle gear. He told me as much as he safely could about that building without breaking military protocol. I don't know what did or didn't happen there that day. I didn't ask. Some things a mother just doesn't need to know or have in her head. All I needed to know was in this second photo. Seeing my son standing beside this purple door I knew he was standing in the very place God knew he was going to be far before he ever got there. I know that on that day and all the other days before and after, my son was safely tucked beneath His wings. God was showing me how very present He is and forever will be in my son's life.

On another occasion, I was prompted out of the blue by the Holy Spirit to go outside and sit. At that time, it was raining, and sitting outside didn't sound super appealing, so I pushed it off for a few minutes, thinking I must have misheard Him. But the Holy Spirit just kept nudging me to go. Honestly, He can be pretty bossy y'all! Finally, I gave in, and I went and sat under the overhang of the roof, and I prayed an annoyed prayer and hastily tried journaling. I wasn't feeling it. I didn't know what I was supposed to be praying for specifically, so after a bit, I just sat in silence with Him. I just sat in the quiet listening to the rain and the drips but not hearing anything from Heaven. I finally said, "Whatever you are doing, God, I want in on it. Whatever the reason I am out here, thank you for including me. I'm going to believe there was a purpose even if I don't know what that is." I honestly thought I had missed whatever it was God was trying to teach or show me. In my journal, I apologized to Him for missing it, and that I would work harder next time to get it. The next day I found out that while I was sitting outside, at that very same time across the globe, my son had been sent out on a mission while on deployment. I had no idea! The whole time I was out there thinking I had missed what God was doing, yet I was actually partnering with Heaven and praying my son through whatever he was facing that day! My son was not alone on that mission. Not only was God with him, but God also had me and my warring angels with him too! This is what it looks like when you pull down Heaven on earth over your sons and daughters. God is always moving and working on our behalf and wanting to partner with our faith and move Heaven in our lives.

There are things He wants to tell us about our children. There is a passage in 1 Samuel chapter nine where Saul is out looking for his father's lost donkeys. In verse nineteen, God tells Samuel that the donkeys Saul is looking for have been found. God told *Samuel* something about what *Saul* was doing. Samuel didn't know the whole story about the donkeys. He just knew what God told him. In that same way, God wants to tell *us* things for and about our *children*. Listen, if God can find and save donkeys, He can certainly find and save your children! Trust Him. He loves them more than we ever could.

I am also going to be honest and tell you there are times I don't have any words. I'm not always as tough as I want to be. There are moments I feel weak, and my heart is so heavy and broken there is nothing left to say or pray. It is during those times when human words are not able to communicate for me; I know that my groans and sighs and lack of words become prayers to Him.

Give ear to my words, O Lord, consider my sighing. Listen to my cry for help, my King and my God, for to you I pray.

PSALM 5:1-2

In this Psalm, we see that when David didn't have any words, he just let his brokenness be the prayer. God is always inclining his ear to us, and He will show up in our brokenness when all we have left is a sigh, a whisper, or a groan.

On Resurrection Sunday, Mary Magdalene runs to the tomb to find Jesus. She had to get to Him! She had to tend to His body! He deserved a proper burial. On Friday, she had watched in horror as they tortured, nailed Him to a cross, and crucified Him. All she had hoped and believed He might be or do had been destroyed as they laid Him in the tomb. This wasn't how it was meant to end. Why didn't somebody do something? Why didn't somebody stop it? She waits through the long hours of Saturday, the weight of death having the final say being much harder to bear than what was endured on Friday. On Friday, the disciples and Mary could still grasp on to hope that somehow He would call ten thousand angels to make all that was wrong right again. Now, as all hope has run out, she stands outside His empty tomb, broken and weeping with a grief so great she was unable to even hold herself upright. Where was He? What had they done with Him? How can this be happening? Then...she hears a word spoken behind her. "Mary." One word, her name. Oh! To hear Him speak your name and have it crash through your darkest moment with the hope of Heaven! She had to go through the Saturday for her to ever realize how amazing that Sunday was going to be. Without the darkest hours of Saturday, Mary and the disciples would never understand the victory of how Heaven doesn't avoid death; it destroys it.

He is never going to leave you. In your darkest moments, when your certainty of who He is collides with the uncertainty of what He is doing, He will speak your name! Sometimes in our broken state, it's easier to find Him and hear Him standing in our presence. In our desperation in realizing we have lost all our human ability to change the situation when all hope has gone, and we are lying flat on the floor surrendered to His will, our tears and our sighs lead us to Heaven's gate. "God, are you still in this?" There in the quiet, you will hear Him call your name. He will bring beauty from our ashes, and from the rubble, He will rebuild our lives.

Praising God in worship while in my brokenness and tears is something I can only give Him here on earth. In Heaven, He will wipe every tear away, and my offering of worship while in the brokenness will be no more. When we sing and worship, our atmosphere changes. We connect with the saints around the Throne of Heaven declaring the majesty and worthiness of our God to be praised. Worship resonates with Heaven. The best example of resonance that I can give you would be the strings of an instrument. If I were to sing over the strings of a baby grand piano or a guitar, the sound from the notes I sing would make those strings come alive and resonate back to me with the very notes I am singing! It's amazing to me that they will make a sound without ever being touched. It's as if they lay waiting and longing to connect and to do the very thing they were created to do. When we sing praises to God, we resonate with Heaven, and Heaven returns to us because Heaven is longing for us to do the very thing we were created to do. The power of His presence as He enters our space makes the enemy flee. If anything can drive back the enemy, it's a song of worship and praise. Satan cannot remain in the presence of praise, so everything he has heaped into our lives to block the vision of power and love of God has to go with satan when we drive him out with praise, and only things of Heaven remain.

You may feel like you have declared and prayed and believed and warred and pressed for a certain promise for your child to come to pass for as long as you can remember and still have not seen any results. But I want to encourage you to keep pressing. In the book of Revelations, there is a really neat passage that explains what is going on with those who are standing around the Throne of Heaven.

Each one had a harp and they were holding golden bowls
full of incense, which are the prayers of the saints.

REVELATIONS 5:8

When I feel like giving up on certain prayers I am pressing in for, I engage my imagination and picture this verse. There are angels around the Throne catching all the prayers of the saints into their bowls. What if that bowl is near full, and all it needs is one last prayer for it to overflow and spill over and out onto God's people? What if that one prayer is the one I am withholding due to weariness or loss of faith and hope? Asking myself that question sends me straight back into prayer. I know that God has always been faithful to me, even when I feel He is distant. I have a history with Him. I know He has never failed me. If there feels like a hush has fallen, and I can't hear Him or see Him moving, I still have to believe He is sovereign. We have to remember that a lot can happen in the still and in the hush. Just because we can't see Him moving doesn't mean He isn't. A lot was happening between Jesus declaring "It is finished!" on the Cross to

"

Satan cannot remain in the presence of praise, so everything he has heaped into our lives to block the vision of power and love of God has to go with satan when we drive him out with praise, and only things of heaven remain.

———————

the moment Mary heard Him call out her name. Come on! He's still on the Throne, and He is still working for our good!

After this, I looked, and there before me was a great multitude that no one could count, from every nation, tribe, people, and language, standing before the throne and before the Lamb. They were wearing white robes and were holding palm branches in their hands.

REVELATION 7:9

There will come a day that we will all be gathered together around the Throne. Until that day, we were created to bring Heaven to earth. We were fashioned to be powerful women of God armed with the weaponry of Heaven. In Christ, we are blessed, chosen, adopted, redeemed, forgiven, sealed to Him, saved, and loved. Knowing we serve a God who loves us that much, how can we not be moved? Let's live a life as ambassadors of Him. Let's make advancements on earth with the power of Heaven through prayer. Let's pray the prayers that bring promises He can partner with and bring them to pass with "Yes, and Amen."

For no matter how many promises God has made, they are "Yes" in Christ, and through him the "Amen" is spoken by us to the glory of God.

2 CORINTHIANS 1:20

Let's line up on the front lines together, praying the scary prayers over our sons and daughters, our country, the nations, and then watch what God can do. Let's live and act and pray from a place of power. He is forever faithful and forever on our side. He will fulfill His promises.

One year for the National Day of Prayer, I was given the high honor of praying over our armed forces from the courthouse lawn. I'm including it here because I thought it might serve as a resource for others to springboard off from. Use this as a place to start. This is only the beginning of how deep and how wide our prayers can reach.

Heavenly Father,

Today we come together to stand in the gap for the American Armed Forces. We lift up every man and woman across this globe, those serving here on U.S soil to those serving with boots on foreign fields, from the one who has served a lifetime, down to the ones with fresh ink still on their contracts, and we declare over them that you are, and forever will be their Commander in Chief.

We lift up the chaplains across the branches. God, would you multiply them so that they would be in plenty supply. Would you create in them a hunger to know you more and a renewed passion to bring your truth and Word and unfailing love and your hope and the redemptive power of the Cross to the troops around them. Bring restoration in times when they are feeling weary and renewed strength to persevere in and carry out the giftings and callings you have placed over their lives.

I stand against the godlessness among the ranks and declare that faith will arise. That men and women who truly know you will rise up and become beacons in the dark places. That they would point others to you and bring the Gospel of Jesus Christ and His hope to those who feel lost, afraid, abandoned, and alone.

I lift up the Commanding Officers across all the branches. Teach them to lead with godly character, integrity, and wisdom. Let them seek your council before passing down orders to those in their command. Let them hear your voice and bring them to understand, as Gideon did, that the trumpet of the Lord cannot fail.

For the families waiting at home during deployment, in the waiting Lord be our comfort, strength, and peace. God, would you teach us how to pray for your military, for our sons and daughters, husbands and wives, mothers and fathers, and all that serve? Would you quicken our spirits to pray your heart and blessings over them? Would you give us dreams in the night and let us be the watchmen on the wall on their behalf? God, teach us how to partner with Heaven for your warriors.

I declare life over the horrific statistic of twenty-two veterans a day losing their battle to suicide—life over every vet battling PTSD. Holy Spirit, would you move in and invade their space. May your truth speak louder in their spirits than any lie that is being repeated in their minds by the enemy. Do what only you can do and what cannot be undone. Release the Holy Spirit fire that consumes and fills them. Let them see that you are bigger than any giant in their way, and your power is greater than anything they have faced, seen, done, or have been through. Bring your resurrection healing power. Restore your battered warriors to wholeness. Bring life, in Jesus' name.

Father, remind every man and woman serving and fighting for the Red, White, and Blue, every morning when their boots hit the boards and every night when they lay to rest that you are forever their strength and shield. Go before and behind them, be their rearguard, hem them in on all sides, cover them above and below, carry them on your wing, be their hedge of protection that no enemy can invade. Keep them safe. Be their lighthouse in the storm and bring them all safe to shore. Bring them home to us whole, body, soul, and spirit. God bless our troops. God bless this nation.

In Jesus' name. Amen.

We were fashioned to be powerful women of God armed with the weaponry of Heaven. Warrior is part of our identity as women. We are designed to be fighters. We are created to be on the front lines. It's time we start running towards the battle line. God has revealed through our children that we were destined to be military moms. Let's use our position, our giftings, our anointings, and our authority as modern-day, Spirit-filled, Shield Maidens to unlock and release "on earth as it is in Heaven" over our children and the generations yet to come. Let's run towards the enemy with the Name and Power of Jesus Christ. It's our time. Let's do this!

THOUGHTS

THOUGHTS